Lucy -

WISH ALL my students

HAD your DRIVE —

Gordon W Nelson

VICTORIA COLLEGE

— 1995 —

Light,
Wind,
and
Structure

This book is published as part of an Alfred P. Sloan Foundation program.

McGraw-Hill Publishing Company

New York   St. Louis   San Francisco
Auckland   Bogotá   Caracas
Hamburg   Lisbon   London   Madrid
Mexico City   Milan   Montreal
New Delhi   Oklahoma City   Paris
San Juan   São Paulo   Singapore
Sydney   Tokyo   Toronto

Light, Wind, and Structure

The Mystery of the Master Builders

Robert Mark

Second Printing, 1990

© 1990 Massachusetts Institute of Technology

This book was set in Galliard by Achorn Graphics and printed and bound by
Halliday Lithograph in the United States of America.

Library of Congress Cataloging-in-Publication Data

Mark, Robert.
    Light, wind, and structure: the mystery of the master builders / Robert Mark.
        p.   cm.—(New liberal arts series)
    Bibliography: p.
    Includes index.
    ISBN 0-07-040403-8
    1. Architecture—Composition, proportion, etc.   2. Structural
engineering.   3. Technical innovations.   I. Title.   II. Series.
NA2760.M365   1990
    721—dc20   89-34736
                                                                    CIP

for Justine and Nicholas

Contents

Series Foreword

The Alfred P. Sloan Foundation's New Liberal Arts (NLA) Program stems from the belief that a liberal education for our time should involve undergraduates in meaningful experiences with technology and with quantitative approaches to problem solving in a wide range of subjects and fields. Students should understand not only the fundamental concepts of technology and how structures and machines function, but also the scientific and cultural settings within which engineers work, and the impacts (positive and negative) of technology on individuals and society. They should be much more comfortable than they are with making calculations, reasoning with numbers and symbols, and applying mathematical and physical models. These methods of learning about nature are increasingly important in more and more fields. They also underlie the process by which engineers create the technologies that exercise such vast influence over all our lives.

The program is closely associated with the names of Stephen White and James D. Koerner, both vice-presidents (retired) of the foundation. Mr. White wrote an internal memorandum in 1980 that led to the launching of the program two years later. In it he argued for quantitative reasoning and technology as "new" liberal arts, not as replacements for the liberal arts as customarily identified, but as liberating modes of thought needed for understanding the technological world in which we now live. Mr. Koerner administered the program for the foundation, successfully leading it through its crucial first four years.

The foundation's grants to 36 undergraduate colleges and 12 universities have supported a large number of seminars, workshops, and symposia on topics in technology and applied mathematics. Many new courses have been developed and existing courses modified at these colleges. Some minors or concentrations in technology studies have been organized. A Resource Center for the NLA Program, located at the State University of New York at Stony Brook, publishes and distributes a monthly newsletter, collects and disseminates syllabi, teaching modules, and other materials prepared at the colleges and universities taking part in the program, and serves in a variety of ways to bring news of NLA activities to all who express interest and request information.

As the program progressed, faculty members who had developed successful new liberal arts courses began to prepare textbooks. Also, a number of the foundation's grants to universities were used to support writing projects of professors—often from engineering departments—who had taught well-attended courses in technology and applied mathematics that had been designed to be accessible to liberal arts undergraduates. It seemed appropriate not only to encourage the preparation of books for such courses, but also to find a way to publish and thereby make available to the widest possible audience the best products of these teaching experiences and writing projects. This is the background with which the foundation approached The MIT Press and the McGraw-Hill Publishing Company about publishing a series of books on the new liberal arts. Their enthusiastic response led to the launching of the New Liberal Arts Series.

The publishers and the Alfred P. Sloan Foundation express their appreciation to the members of the Editorial Advisory Board for the New Liberal Arts Series: John G. Truxal, Distinguished Teaching Professor, Department of Technology and Society, State University of New York, Stony Brook, Chairman; Joseph Bordogna, Alfred Fitler Moore Professor and Dean, School of Engineering and Applied Science, University of Pennsylvania; Robert W. Mann, Whitaker Professor of Biomedical Engineering, Massachusetts Institute of Technology; Merritt Roe Smith, Professor of the History of Technology, Massachusetts Institute of Technology; J. Ronald Spencer, Associate Academic Dean and

Lecturer in History, Trinity College; and Allen B. Tucker, Jr., Professor of Computer Science, Bowdoin College. In developing this new publication program, The MIT Press has been represented by Frank P. Satlow and the McGraw-Hill Publishing Company by Eric M. Munson.

Samuel Goldberg
Program Officer
Alfred P. Sloan Foundation

Preface

Paul Goldberger, the architecture critic of the *New York Times,* has observed in several recent articles that "our culture has shown more interest in the field of architecture than ever before." That interest is reflected by the publication in just two years (1985 and 1986) of four major texts devoted to the general history of architecture and intended for use in college-level survey courses. The authors of these texts recognize the central role of technology in large-scale architecture. Yet, with their traditional emphasis on formal stylistic development, symbolism, and iconography, they fail to maintain a consistent focus on building technology or on the crucial *interaction* of structure and style in historic architecture.

The present work is not intended to supplant these general texts, nor for that matter does it attempt to present a coherent account of the sweep of Western architectural history. Rather, it deals mainly with three historic eras that witnessed the development of new large-scale building types that retain great influence in architectural planning up to the present day. The application of modern engineering tools has clarified the technological underpinning of these developments and provided new insights into the design techniques employed by the early builders. Hence, another theme of the present work is the reinterpretation of technological precedents that are often misunderstood in contemporary architecture. It is hoped that this book, when used together with the general texts, will provide a stronger technological focus on all of architectural history as well as a basis for more rational criticism of contemporary design.

Much of the material derives from a seminar offered annually at Princeton and usually co-taught by the author and an architectural historian. Begun a little more than a decade ago with a focus on Gothic structure, the seminar now treats issues of structure and style from the whole history of architecture. The results of related research have been published in a wide spectrum of journals, including the *Annals of the New York Academy of Science, American Scientist, Art Bulletin, Experimental Mechanics, Interdisciplinary Science Reviews,* the *Journal of the Society of Architectural Historians, Scientific American, The Sciences,* and *Technology and Culture,* which makes them difficult to collect by anyone working in a single field of scholarship. Some of these new materials have already found use in seminars for visiting faculty sponsored by the Alfred P. Sloan Foundation and the National Endowment for the Humanities and held at Princeton during the summers of 1985–1988. They were also used in a University of Michigan colloquium held during the spring of 1988 (the colloquium was jointly sponsored by departments of archaeology, architecture and planning, art history, and engineering), and they provided the basis for "The Mystery of the Master Builders," a "Nova" program first broadcast by PBS in March 1988.

The text is aimed at the general reader as well as at students of architecture and architectural history. An effort has been made to minimize jargon, but the nature of the subject demands that some technological ideas and terms be used. These are introduced in a simple manner in chapter 2. Sources of more detailed reference information are referred to in the notes. Architectural and technical terms are defined throughout the text, in illustrations, and in a glossary. Both the metric and the English system of units are generally used, but for the sake of clarity some of the drawings display units in only one system.

Important contributions to this work have been made by a number of my present and former colleagues at Princeton, including Kirk D. Alexander, David P. Billington, Slobodan Ćurčić, Michael Davis, Robert Gutman, Jean-Herve Prévost, Robert Scanlon, and Harry Titus, and by other scholars, including Sheila Bonde, William W. Clark, Lynn T. Courtenay, Harold Dorn, Joel Herschman, William Loerke, William L. MacDonald, Clark

Maines, Christopher Mark, Claudia Marchitiello Mark, Rowland Richards, Jr., Elwin Robison, and Leonard Van Gulick, to all of whom I am greatly indebted. Some of my former students (in architecture, art history, and engineering) also took part in these studies, including several with whom I have collaborated in publication: Yun-Sheng Huang, Paul Hutchinson, Anne Westagard Stokes, and William Taylor.

I wish to express my gratitude to the National Endowment for the Humanities, the Alfred P. Sloan Foundation, and the Andrew W. Mellon Foundation for sponsoring research and education programs of which this research was a part. I am indebted also to the John Simon Guggenheim Foundation for the granting of a fellowship in 1982–83 which enabled me to become familiar with and to photograph the fabric of many of the ancient sites, and to the National Science Foundation for a Scholar's Grant in 1983–84 which provided further assistance with these studies.

Finally, I am most grateful to the readers of The MIT Press and to William W. Clark, Lynn T. Courtenay, and Sergio Sanabria for editorial suggestions; to Robert Bork, Yun-Sheng Huang, David Lauer, Elizabeth Newman, and Valerio Simini for line drawings and computer-generated illustrations; and to J. Weyman Williams for producing print conversions from my color slides.

Photographs for which credits are not given are by the author.

Light,
Wind,
and
Structure

I

Problems of Technological Interpretation in Historic Architecture

The Opera House in Sydney stands high over the harbor like a great ship, its sail-like roof shells of concrete raised on a terraced platform. Yet its appearance betrays none of its ideological foundations. The project was begun in 1957 when the Danish architect Jorn Utzon submitted a series of freehand sketches of the roof shells to an international design competition and won the commission. The opera house finally opened in 1973, nine years behind schedule and at a cost that exceeded the original estimate of $10 million by more than $130 million—mostly because of an inappropriate notion of "honest" structural design.[1]

In the early stages of the project, Utzon and his structural engineer, Ove Arup, decided that the arching, pointed shells, which were to reach as high as 60 meters (197 feet) above their base and to be inlaid with ceramic panels, should be honestly self-supporting. In other words, the roof shells—whose form was determined primarily on the basis of aesthetic, sculptural considerations—would have to sustain the considerable forces of gravity and wind without support from any additional structural framing underneath. It would not be enough for the shells (composed of segments from a sphere 75 m [246 ft] in radius) to be aesthetically appealing; form would have to serve function. There would be no lazy, unworking shapes and no hidden supports.

1.1
Jorn Utzon and Ove Arup: Opera
House, Sydney, 1973. (photo: WGBH/
Nova)

And so tens of millions of dollars were spent for years of engineering and computing time to produce a design for a vastly intricate, self-supporting, prestressed-concrete roof system.

Still more money went into reconstructing the terraced platform on which the shells were to rest after the designers found that the one originally constructed, in an attempt to make up for lost time and to schedule an even flow of work, would not hold up the roof. A simpler and far less expensive structural system, composed of hidden steel trusses, could have been used to support the sculptural shells, but the designers rejected this option and chased after their vision of technological morality—which Arup defended with a specious historical argument: "The cost, the length of time it is taking to complete, the use to which the building will be put, and so on have been discussed almost *ad nauseam*. As a consequence, the challenge, the excitement and the technical problems encountered in what must be one of the most complex structures ever built, have become obscured. Sydney Opera House is not the kind of building which often comes within the orbit of the structural engineer. It is an adventure in building. It is not really of this age and in concept is more appropriate to an autocratic rule of a former era."[2]

Although the Sydney Opera House has come to symbolize the tension between technology and art that exists in much of contemporary architecture,[3] Eero Saarinen—the architect who dominated the jury that awarded the Opera House commission to Utzon—had already been the author of a similar technological fiasco. His Kresge Auditorium, constructed on the campus of the Massachusetts Institute of Technology in 1955, was also conceived for visual effect without regard for structural imperatives—a fact that became painfully evident during its construction. Yet this was not the consensus of contemporary commentators. Even so astute a critic as Allan Temko thought the shell form attributable to "its absolute structural premise." "The auditorium," he went on, "can be recognized as closer to the 'correct' structural theory of Nervi . . . than to the structural rhetoric of [Wright's] Guggenheim Museum." And Saarinen himself did nothing to clarify the issue when he commented that "in developing the design of this building, we felt very strongly guided by Mies's principle of architecture—of consistent structure and a forthright expression of that structure."[4]

The cast-in-place concrete shell roof of the Kresge Auditorium, with its span of 49 m (160 ft) between supports, has the

form of an equilateral spherical triangle, comprising one-eighth of the full surface of a sphere with a radius of 34 m (112 ft).[5] The shell was originally intended to be of uniform thickness and to be supported only at its three corners by massive foundations. But deformation, caused by large bending forces along the outer edges after the removal of the temporary centering over which the concrete had been poured, demanded that reinforcement be added to the shell and that the window mullions be redesigned to provide edge support. Even with the modifications, additional long-time deformations, combined with the effect of movements caused by changes in temperature, hastened the deterioration of the roof and of the elaborate and costly lead covering that was applied to it when some of the problems first became apparent. With every heavy rain the auditorium flooded. More critically, the steel reinforcement within the shell corroded so badly from continual wetting that it began to lose strength. In 1979 the entire building had to be closed for more than a year to allow major reconstruction.

Tall office buildings are not immune to similar problems of design. With its great height, the form of the modern skyscraper might be expected to be influenced by the effect of wind. Indeed, as will be shown in chapter 4, even the external profile of the much lower and relatively heavy (compared with modern frame construction) High Gothic cathedral resulted in part from structural impairment caused by high winds. And although a response to wind forces is reflected in the form of at least some tall modern buildings (as exemplified by the John Hancock Center in Chicago, discussed in chapter 6), it does not appear to have been a primary consideration in the planning (by I. M. Pei and his chief designer, Henry N. Cobb) of the John Hancock Tower in Boston, an extremely slender 60-story steel-frame building clad in mirrored glass. The cladding was intended to reflect the downtown scene and to allow the tower, the tallest structure in the city, to fade into the background. In 1971, when the building was still under construction, the windows started to fall out; by the summer of 1973 almost a quarter of the glass had been lost. Occupancy had to be postponed for $3\frac{1}{2}$ years while extensive structural modifications were undertaken, which included stiffening the building's frame against twisting deformation. As a further palliative for excessive motion in high winds, tuned-mass dampers (huge moving weights high up in the structure, controlled by sophisticated electronic sensors) were installed. And all of the original windows needed to be replaced.

Notwithstanding its checkered genesis and the persistence of problems with the windows (which still required vigilant monitoring), the American Institute of Architects cited the Hancock Tower in 1977 as an "outstanding architectural achievement": ". . . as an object on the skyline, it catches the sun, reflects the sky, and acts as an effective new landmark for downtown Boston. . . . It is perhaps the most handsome reflective glass building; history may show it to be the last great example of the species."[6] There was no mention by the jury of any of the building's expensive technological problems. But even more distressing than the granting of the award is the fact that the collective "technological blind spot" of that distinguished group of architectural practitioners corresponds to the trend of much current architectural literature.[7]

Although almost every observer would maintain that large-scale monumental architecture represents a fusion of artistic, cultural, societal, and technological motives, the role of technology in the design process is, more often than not, neglected or confused in the very treatises by which architects set great store. In some cases technology is even vilified, as in the recent award-winning text by the theorist Alberto Pérez-Gómez, who laments the post-Newtonian scientific "rejection of myth, poetry, and art as legitimate and primary forms of knowledge" that led to the "evils brought about by the transformation of architectural theory into an instrument of technological domination that excluded metaphysics."[8] In this romantic context, where consideration of environmental forces (such as gravity) would seem only to hinder design creativity, the late-eighteenth-century hypothetical projects of Etienne-Louis Boullée and Claude-Nicolas Ledoux are treated as heroic. Both men had successful architectural practices, but today they are known almost exclusively for their visionary designs. Boullée's projects particularly, with their haunting imagery as in the cenotaph for Isaac Newton, were of such huge scale as to be entirely unbuildable. Yet, according to Pérez-Gómez, "It is significant that the symbolic intentionality of these two architects could no longer be embodied in three-dimensional buildings. . . . Thus for the first time in the history of European architecture . . . architectural intentions had to be expressed almost exclusively through theoretical projects that obviously did not fit into the new, essentially prosaic world of industrial society."[9]

Such discourse ignores the evidence of resolute programs of industrial-scale building in "pre-scientific" eras well before the

John Hancock
Observatory

1.4

*John Hancock Tower, reflecting Trinity
Church.*

1.5

*Etienne-Louis Boullée: project for a
cenotaph for Isaac Newton, 1784.*

seventeenth century.[10] Nor does it account for the many instances where stunning architectural style derived from attention to structural need, as in the case of the stepped rings around the bases of ancient domes or the flying buttresses of Gothic cathedrals. And in view of the attendant disdain for the "new industrial society," it is ironic that architectural fantasy is now most likely found in what *New York Times* reporter Joseph Giovannini has termed the "giant architectural logos" of American corporations: "flamboyant headquarters buildings . . . representing a historic departure from the unornamented, sometimes anonymous, glass-box office structures of the postwar generation."[11] These "architectural logos," according to the sociologist Robert Gutman, are an "indication of the . . . recognition that architecture is an art . . . that has economic value and carries social value. Buildings that are aesthetically pleasing are admired for the pleasure they give and also because buildings so endowed are more likely to attract tenants and yield higher rents."[12] In this milieu, it is not surprising that some well-known architects have begun to accept commissions that limit their participation to no more than the artistic design of a building's facade. Indeed, as Gutman goes on to explain,

in terms of the theory of architecture, it has become easier for architects to accommodate themselves to a more confined role because of the spread of the modernist doctrine in the arts which argues that the aesthetic dimension is autonomous. Architecture resisted this doctrine longer than the other arts, because architecture, unlike painting or literature, seemed to have a connection to building function and use which was impossible to sever. However, contemporary efficiencies in the system of building production and construction technology [and] a system of practice in which sponsors or other firms are available to relieve the artist-architect from the burden of dealing with technical issues [have] now liberated architects along with other artists.[13]

Similar inconsistencies in relating the connection of physical building to the art of architecture are encountered even in the writings of an architectural theorist who was also a celebrated practitioner and who professed great admiration for technology. "The engineer's aesthetic and architecture are two things that march together and follow from one another: the one [engineering] being now in full height, the other being in an unhappy state of retrogression," Le Corbusier wrote in 1923 in *Towards a New Architecture*, perhaps the most influential work on architecture of this century.[14] Even so, according to Le Corbusier, the engineer merely achieves "harmony" through mathematical calculation, and it is *only* the architect who "by his arrangement of forms realizes an order which is pure creation of the spirit." "Architecture," Le Corbusier continues, "is the masterly, correct and magnificent play of masses brought together in light. . . . cubes, cones, spheres, cylinders or pyramids are the great primary forms which light reveals to advantage. . . . it is for this reason that these are *beautiful forms, the most beautiful forms*. . . . Egyptian, Greek or Roman architecture is an architecture of prisms, cubes and cylinders, pyramids or spheres."[15]

Le Corbusier's theories of architectural design would seem to derive more from his early experience as a cubist painter than from his having observed large structures—such as the 300 m (980 ft) tall Eiffel Tower (constructed in Paris in 1887–1889), whose profile is based on a *parabolic* form determined from internal distributions of forces caused by wind loadings.[16] In point of fact, simple geometric forms are often inappropriate for large-scale structures.

Evidently, Le Corbusier was also much influenced by photographs of American industrial buildings, which abound in *Towards a New Architecture*. "Insofar as the International Style was copied from American industrial prototypes and models," Reyner Banham observed, "it must be the first architectural movement in the history of the art based almost exclusively on photographic evidence rather than on the ancient and previously unavoidable techniques of personal inspection and measured drawing."[17] As Banham also notes, there were technological disadvantages in this: "While European flat roofs may indeed have leaked as often as was claimed, the American industrial ones generally did not. . . . A properly detailed and constructed flat roof can be as staunch as any pitched roof. . . . Many of [the modernist roofs] were purely formalistic imitations of structures that had never been studied at first hand. Their designers had not seen the originals and had no opportunity to examine and understand how they should be designed, detailed, and constructed."[18]

Rather than search for new styles based on appropriate, elegant structure (as in the case of the Eiffel Tower), modern architects often based their forms on the *notion* of a "machine aesthetic." Cylindrical concrete grain elevators, for example, served as the models for new styles of urban dwellings. More recently, the machine aesthetic has been manifested in buildings that appear to be structural *tours de force* but are in fact merely expensive displays of structural elaboration—for example, the Centre Pompidou in Paris, completed in 1976.

1.6
Richard Rogers and Renzo Piano:
Centre Pompidou, Paris, 1971.

1.7
Foreground: 1926 Fiat 509 roadster.
Background: Temple of Poseidon, Paes-
tum, Italy. (photo: WGBH/Nova)

Le Corbusier also misinterpreted the technological basis of earlier monumental architecture—even the structure of a classical Greek temple. Multiple photographs of temples are juxtaposed with those of early-twentieth-century sports cars in *Towards a New Architecture* to suggest parallel technical progress. (Figure 1.7 is based on Le Corbusier's juxtaposition.) The most basic structural analysis will show, however, that the "prismatic" posts and lintels adopted by the ancient Greeks from earlier timber structures could lead only to a technological dead end.[19] Unreinforced masonry has almost no tensile (pulling) strength. The stone columns (posts) supporting mostly compression loadings (causing the individual stones to be pushed together) are fine. The lintels, however, which are bent by the effect of gravity, are subject to appreciable tensile forces along their lower edges, even if the supporting columns are relatively closely spaced. This problem seems to have been well understood by the ancient designers. The archaeologist J. J. Coulton describes how the architect of the "colossal" temple of Zeus Olympia, constructed at Agrigento, Sicily, in the first half of the fifth century B.C., eschewed the classical post-and-lintel temple structure to avoid the problem of the lintel, replacing it in all but its exterior form with load-bearing walls of ashlar.[20] But that building was exceptional. Unlike that of early automobiles, the form of the classical temple described by Le Corbusier was developed almost entirely through fashion. None of this depreciates the aesthetic triumph of the temple; still, it is important to emphasize that the temple was intended to be appreciated primarily for its sculptural exterior form and its relationship to the site, rather than for the kind of interior spatial effect associated with later structural invention.[21]

Interpreting the technological underpinnings of the far more complex buildings of later eras is even more fraught with pitfalls. For example, the design techniques employed by early builders to create new forms to cover vast interior spaces—particularly the temples and baths of Imperial Rome and the light, soaring structures of the Gothic cathedral at the turn of the twelfth century—have persistently puzzled historians. The enigma surrounding the design of these buildings is all the more appreciated when one realizes that the first gleamings of modern analytical structural theory are found in Galileo's notebooks from the late sixteenth century.

With the wide dissemination of written design rules and the publication of drawings of existing buildings, beginning in the fifteenth century, empirical rules of construction were increasingly codified; but it was not until the middle of the nineteenth century, with the introduction of new construction materials and far greater loadings than in pre-industrial eras, that scientific methods began to be used more commonly in structural design.[22] Indeed, the general application of analytical techniques to design is largely a development of the late nineteenth century. There is not even the slightest possibility that any analytical theory was available to the early builders; hence, other explanations for their successes must be sought.

The problems of historical-technological interpretation identified in recent architectural literature and in the rationale for contemporary practice thus relate to misbegotten notions of "structural honesty," of the past use of "unlimited resources for monumental architecture," of the appropriateness of primary geometric forms in architectural design, and of technological imperatives impeding architectural creativity and thereby creating the "need for liberation of the contemporary artist-architect from the burden of dealing with technical issues."[23] Outside of these polemics, there remains the "mystery" of how the early master builders created great architecture without resort to modern analytical theory.

Much of the misinterpretation derives from the apparent complexity of past monuments. Fortunately, experimental and computer-modeling techniques capable of reliably analyzing such complex forms have become available in recent decades. The application of these techniques to questions of historic building—particularly in the context of information from primary documents, from archaeological examination, and from formal analysis—has added an important new dimension to historical study. It has greatly increased our understanding of both technological and aesthetic innovation, and it has led to a reassessment of the theories of pre-scientific design that have misinformed so much architectural writing.

As will be seen in chapter 5, the question of "structural honesty" in contemporary architecture is brilliantly illuminated by an understanding of the basis of Christopher Wren's design for the dome of St. Paul's Cathedral. The economic limitations of past eras are highlighted by new insights into ancient technology (chapter 3) and by the documented periods of inactivity between medieval building campaigns (chapter 4). Structural modification of primary geometric forms in order to preserve stability has been a common practice throughout the history of architecture, and the heightened perception of the interaction of technology and style in individual buildings, as well as within sequences of buildings from every era, serves to undermine the idea of "liberating" the architect from practical issues. Furthermore, as will be argued in chapter 6, these new insights into monumental structures of the past that have provided influential design precedents can invigorate a now-neglected field of criticism of contemporary architecture.

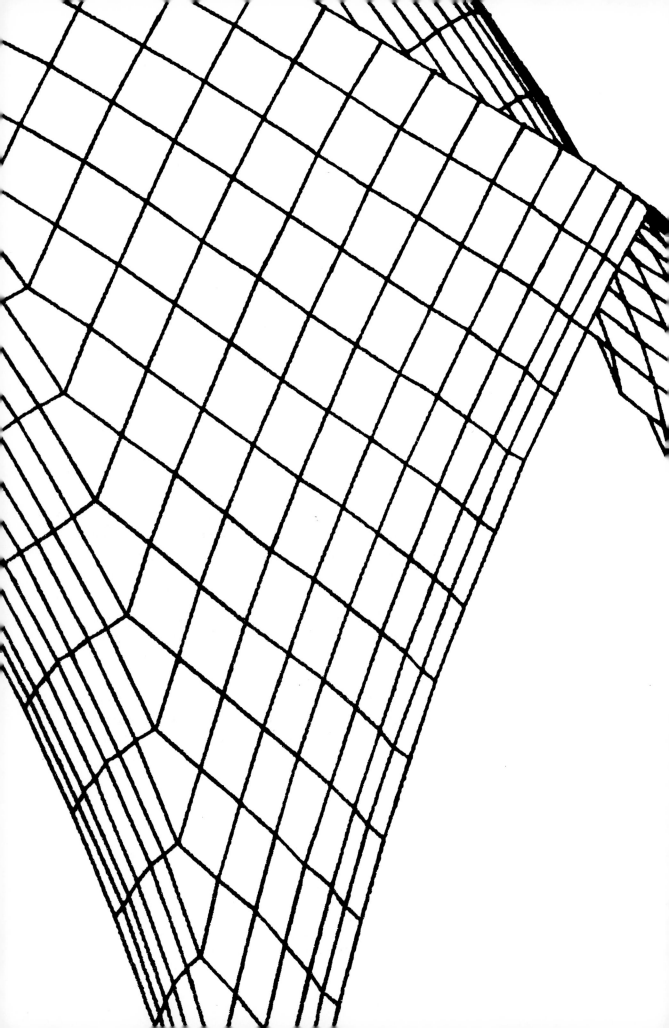

2

The Technology of Light, Wind, and Structure

Besides meeting the demands of formal and societal requirements, the design of all large-scale historic buildings was influenced by either real or perceived structural limitations. Because it is by far the most obvious of all the applied loadings, supporting the dead weight of the building itself would have been the primary concern of the early builders. The response to the effects of high winds, of dislocations during construction, of differential (uneven) settlement of foundations, of thermal expansion associated with the curing of large masses of concrete and the heating of portions of a structure by the sun, and of dynamic ground motions associated with earthquakes requires far more sophisticated understanding than simply supporting downward-acting weight. Nevertheless, in the following chapters it will be shown that the structural forms used by the Romans in their relatively heavy construction with unreinforced concrete were influenced by their understanding of the effects of thermally induced forces, and that wind became a major factor in design as stone buildings grew taller and lighter during the Gothic era.

A simple introductory text on structural behavior is James E. Gordon's *Structures, or Why things don't fall down* (Plenum, 1981). On light and optics, see David S. Falk, Dieter R. Brill, and David G. Stork, *Seeing the Light* (Harper and Row, 1986). For further information on wind loading, see Emil Simiu and Robert H. Scanlon, *Wind Effects on Structures*, second edition (Wiley-Interscience, 1986). On dimensional analysis, see P. W. Bridgeman, *Dimensional Analysis* (Yale University Press, 1931). On physical modeling, see James W. Dally and William F. Riley, *Experimental Stress Analysis*, second edition (McGraw-Hill, 1978). On numerical (computer) modeling, see Robert D. Cook, *Concepts and Applications of Finite Element Analysis*, second edition (Wiley, 1981).

Providing sources of natural light was also an important consideration for the early designers. The paleontologist Stephen Jay Gould even suggested the possibility that the plans of the great Gothic churches were derived from the lighting requirements of building at a new, larger scale.[1]

This chapter offers a brief introduction to the physics of light and of wind, and to the modern techniques of structural analysis that enable us to gain insights into the technological intentions of the early designers. With these insights, we may also address issues such as that posed by Gould. The section on light follows the necessarily far longer introductory treatment of structure, which comprises subsections on structural forces; deformation, stress, and strain; strength and stability; building materials; loadings, including wind effects; scaling; and structural modeling. The chapter is designed to provide the modern technological underpinning for the historical studies that follow. A few elementary algebraic relationships are presented, but these need not discourage the "nonmathematical" reader; the arguments are generally presented in qualitative terms as well, usually with help from diagrams and graphs.

Structure

Structural Forces

For a structure to maintain its integrity (equilibrium) when loadings are applied to it, resisting forces within the structure must counteract the applied loadings. For example, if a cable used in a hoist lifts a weight, the top of the cable will be subjected to *tension* (a stretching force) equal to the sum of the weight lifted and the weight of the cable. An upright stone buttress, as illustrated in figure 2.1a, undergoes *compression* (a pushing force) from its own weight. At the top of the stone the compression force is zero (if the pinnacle's weight is neglected); at the base the compressive force must equal the total weight of the buttress.

The inclined applied force *F* (which might be transmitted by an adjacent flying buttress) acting on the buttress in figure 2.1b can be *resolved* into vertical and horizontal *components* of force; that is, the inclined force can be replaced by two imaginary forces that together have the same effect as the single force. This is done geometrically: If the length of line *F* represents the magnitude and direction of the inclined force, the lengths of the vertical and horizontal legs of the right triangle formed with *F* as hypotenuse give the magnitudes of these components. The vertical force component *V* adds to the compression from the buttress's weight, and

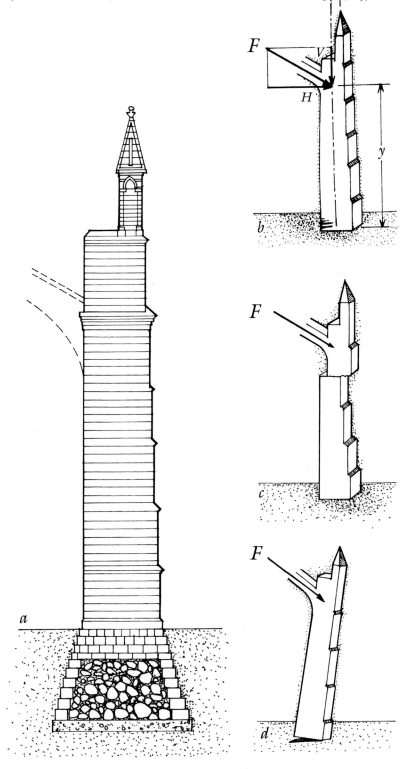

2.1

Buttress forces and failure modes: (a) upright buttress and footing; (b) buttress with applied loading, illustrating vertical and horizontal force components and cracking caused by bending; (c) shear failure; (d) overturning.

the horizontal force component H subjects the upright buttress also to internal *bending* and *shear* forces. Under bending, the loaded side of the buttress will stretch. If the internal tension is excessive, cracking will develop first at the base of the buttress (figure 2.1b). The unloaded side of the buttress shown in figure 2.1b, on the other hand, will experience only additional compression from bending. The effect of excessive shear is illustrated in figures 2.1c and 2.2. A combination of these internal forces is usually present in all structures.

Reactions are the internal forces that provide support to a loaded structure. For example, the supporting reaction at the base of the buttress in figure 2.1a is a vertical compressive force equal to the total weight of the buttress. In the example of figure 2.1b, there must be three reactions acting at the base of the buttress: a vertical compression equal to the sum of the weight of the buttress and the vertical force component V, a bending moment equal to the product of the horizontal force component H and the height of the force above the base of the buttress y, and a shearing force of magnitude H. If the influence of the pinnacle atop the outside edge of the buttress in figure 2.1b were also to be taken into account, the pinnacle's weight would be added into the vertical reaction; it would also add to the bending an amount equal to the product of the pinnacle's weight and the offset distance from its center of gravity to the center line of the upright buttress, x, but the weight of the pinnacle would have no effect on the internal shear.

The *conditions of support* achieved by the foundations affect the reactions greatly. For example, the base of the buttress illustrated in figure 2.1b provides *fixity* against vertical movement, horizontal sliding, and rotation. If the buttress were supported only by a *hinge* that allowed rotation, it would need another reactive force (such as a compression strut at a second point of support) to maintain equilibrium by preventing rotation and overturning.

The *footings*, which provide support to the superstructure, distribute the building's reactions to the underlying soil or rock. Footings need to be broad-based enough so that the pressure on the soil beneath a footing—the *bearing pressure* (equal to the total loading on the footing divided by the area of the footing base)—is not so great as to give rise to excessive soil movement (*settlement*). A large amount of settlement is not usually serious as long as it is uniform; however, *differential settlement*—the uneven settle-

| | Bearing pressure | |
Subsoil	metric ton/m²	ton/ft²
Massive rock	1,000	100
Compacted gravel	100	10
Loose gravel	60	6
Sand	20	2
"Hard" clays	40	4
"Soft" clays	10	1

ment of separate portions of a building—can lead to critical dislocations and fractures within the building fabric. Representative bearing pressures, as recommended in modern design codes for a wide range of subsoil types, are given in table 2.1.

Rigid reinforced-concrete footings are now placed under columns and bearing walls to evenly distribute building loadings to the subsoil and to reduce bearing pressures to prescribed levels. Before this type of modern footing came into use (late in the nineteenth century), stepped-block stone footings similar to the one illustrated in figure 2.1a were used to accomplish the same end.[2] And since the bearing pressure at the base of a splayed, stepped footing is usually of lower magnitude than the compression near its narrower top, the stone used for the lower portion of the footing (which is confined by the soil around it) need not be as high-quality as the masonry above. Early builders seem to have understood this; instead of cut stone, rubble was often used at the footing base.[3]

Deformation, Stress, and Strain

Loadings cause all structures to undergo *deformation*; compression causes shortening, tension causes stretching, and bending produces curvature wherein one side of a structure is stretched while the other side is shortened. In most structures, deformation is not directly observable (the deformation caused by bending illustrated in figure 2.1b is much exaggerated); yet it can be measured with sensitive instruments. The *stiffness* of a structure, a measure of its resistance to deformation, is determined by its overall configuration and by the physical properties of its constructional materials. For example, a structure in steel would be 3 times stiffer than the same structure in aluminum and about 20 times stiffer than the same structure in construction-grade timber. Under ordinary, short-time loading conditions, building materials can be considered *elastic*; that is, when the loading is removed, they return to their original form, as a rubber band does. Extreme loadings and loadings of long duration, though, produce additional permanent deformation, a phenomenon known as *creep*.

Stress is a measure of the local intensity of force acting within a structure. For a simple, concentrically loaded strut, the stress is found merely by dividing the total force carried by the strut by its cross-sectional area. For example, if a lightweight strut (i.e., the weight of the strut itself is negligible) with a cross-section of 1 cm² (0.155 in²) is compressed by a force of 100 kg (220 lb), the compressive stress within the strut is given by the following equation:

$$100 \text{ kg/1 cm}^2 = 100 \text{ kg/cm}^2 \text{ (1,420 psi)}$$

In the same manner, tension forces give rise to *tensile stress* and shear forces to *shear stress*. Bending, which is normally accompanied by tension, compression, and shear, can give rise to all three types of stress.

Strain is a measure of local deformation within a structure. *Tension, compression*, and *shear* strains generally accompany tension, compression, and shear stresses. If the physical properties of the structural material are established and the stress is determined from an analysis, the strain is easily found. Conversely, if the physical properties are established and the strains are known, the stresses are easily calculated. Hence, *electric strain gauges,* which measure strain in a full-scale structure or a small-scale model (as described below in the subsection on modeling), can also be used to determine stress.

Strength and Stability

The *strength* of a material is defined as the level of stress that causes the material to fail. Structural damage occurs when the stress within a structure exceeds the material strength. The compression (crushing) strengths of many building materials are much higher than their tension (tearing) strengths; for example, the tensile strength of masonry is usually about two orders of magnitude less than its compressive strength. Yet cracking in masonry construction caused by tension accompanying bending, such as that illustrated in figure 2.1b, is not necessarily catastrophic. Complete collapse, or *structural instability*, occurs only when the crack at the base of the buttress has propagated across the entire section, as illustrated in figure 2.1d. The stability of the buttress against overturning now depends on its weight and its base dimensions. A heavier buttress whose base is splayed out is more resistant against the overturning caused by the horizontal force component H acting at the top of the buttress than a lighter, narrower buttress. Moreover, if a buttress begins to overturn, the weight of the pinnacle pressing down on the buttress's outer edge will not help in righting it. If the pinnacle is to add to the overall stability of the buttress, it must be placed inboard.

Another type of structural instability can occur in a slender strut or column. Because such a member is rarely exactly "true" in all dimensions, accidental bending stresses will accompany the nominal compressive stress, and the combined effect the two types of stress can induce a mode of failure known as *column buckling*. Avoiding this behavior is a most important design consideration for slender structures of timber, of metal, and of reinforced concrete, but column buckling is rarely encountered in more massive masonry construction.

Building Materials

The most common materials used in early construction are timber, masonry (of stone or fired brick), and unreinforced concrete. *Timber* differs from the others in its ability to accept tension, although the tensile capacity of a timber structure is often limited by the strength of its joints in shear rather than by the cross-sections of the members. Hence timber strengths (in both tension and compression), which range from about 150 kg/cm² (2,100 psi) for soft woods to about 400 kg/cm² (5,700 psi) for hard woods (including the oaks used almost universally in Northern European structures), can serve only as a guide for design. Both dimensional stability and the properties of timber are sensitive to changes in moisture content, and long-time loadings produce creep.[4] Also, because of the natural growth variation of its internal structure, timber (even from a common source) is notorious for exhibiting a broad range of properties and for being anisotropic (that is, displaying different structural responses depending on the direction of the applied forces relative to the alignment of its grain).[5]

Granite, limestone, and sandstone are the major constituents of *stone* masonry construction. Because of its general availability, its endurance, and its relatively easy workability, limestone is the stone most commonly used for load-bearing walls and piers. The

strength of all stone in compression, but especially that of limestone, is variable. It is similar to wood in being sensitive to such
factors as the relationship between the stone's orientation in its
natural bed and the direction in which forces are applied to it in a
building. The compressive strength of limestone ranges from a
maximum of about 2,000 kg/cm^2 (28,000 psi) to a minimum of
200 kg/cm^2 (2,800 psi). The range of tensile strengths for all stone
is an order of magnitude lower than the range of compressive
values, and these tensile strengths, in turn, are usually an order of
magnitude greater than the tensile strength of the mortar used as
grout between the surfaces of the ashlar.[6] To understand the performance of masonry, therefore, it is important to give attention
to the general properties of mortars.

Most pre-modern *mortars* were basically composed of pure
lime or of lime-and-sand mixtures. Such mortars are not hydraulic
(i.e., they do not set under water), and they are often described,
erroneously, as taking anywhere from months to centuries to dry.
In fact, lime mortar passes through two separate stages: setting
and carbonation. Pure lime mortar paste is said to be "set" when
all the water has evaporated into the atmosphere or has been absorbed into the surrounding masonry blocks.[7] The time taken by
this process varies with the amount of excess water, the relative
humidity, the absorption rates of the stone, and the mass of the
construction. Lime mortar is described as "slow-setting" only in
contrast with modern Portland cement, which will set in about 10
hours. Lime mortar may take days or perhaps weeks to dry, but
not years. Carbonation, in comparison, is a very slow process. The
set mortar paste, calcium hydroxide, reacts with carbon dioxide to
form calcium carbonate, the basic constitutent of limestone.
Under ordinary circumstances, the process is slow because of the
small amount of carbon dioxide available in the atmosphere. In
addition, diffusion of carbon dioxide deep into the masonry beyond a thin surface of carbonated mortar occurs very slowly if
at all.

Lime mortar that is only set is not very strong, even in compression. However, neither the strength of the mortar nor that of
the masonry blocks is as important as the properties of their combined construction. The strengths and the deformation characteristics of masonry construction are difficult to predict, since those of
the constituent elements are not well known. Indeed, test results
on discrete samples of materials are not accurate indicators of the
behavior of the same materials when they are used in large quan-

tities in buildings. Studies of masonry walls loaded perpendicular to the mortar bed have shown that mortar can survive under conditions where its simple crushing strength is exceeded by as much as 300 percent.[8] In my own observations of masonry construction, I have never discerned a failure initiated by crushing, only distress caused by tension cracking or by shear (as illustrated in figure 2.2).

Unlike the simple lime mortars produced by adding water to a mixture of quicklime and sand, cements consisting of dark volcanic sand and lime (or of limestone and clays or shale burned in a furnace and then pulverized, as in today's Portland cement) set by combining chemically with water. Large batches of these so-called hydraulic cements cure relatively rapidly even when kept

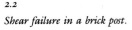

2.2
Shear failure in a brick post.

wet. Thus, Roman pozzolana cement (named after the town of Pozzuoli, near Naples, where the volcanic ash used in its manufacture was discovered) could be used for the massive primary structural elements of large buildings as well as for underwater construction. The early compressive strengths of hydraulic cements are also far superior to that of lime mortars.[9] One must remain cautious, however, in characterizing the resistance of any unreinforced concrete—whether it is used as mortar within masonry or as a solid mass—to cracking caused by tensile forces. Although modern concrete made with controlled-cured, high-quality Portland cement exhibits measurable tensile strength, in modern reinforced-concrete design its tensile capacity is still taken to be nil. Experience has dictated that reinforcing steel is always needed in the regions of a concrete structure where tension is present.

The substitution of kiln-fired *brick* for stone in masonry construction, other things being equal, makes little difference in overall structural behavior. Yet on-site construction would have been simplified by employing a more uniform building product than was available with pre-industrial finished stone. Probably to save on both time and cost, late Roman builders, especially in the provinces, often used brick with much thicker mortar beds in conjunction with weak lime mortars that considerably reduced the overall strength of the masonry. Fairly thick mortar beds, which in Hadrian's time were about $\frac{1}{2}$ to $\frac{2}{3}$ the thickness of the brick (brick being typically about 6 cm, or 2.4 inches, thick), were later enlarged to as much as $1\frac{2}{3}$ of the brick's thickness—a system of construction used for the buttressing of the Hagia Sophia in Constantinople in the sixth century. As will be explained in chapter 3, this detail of construction, probably more than any other factor, led to the failure of that building's first dome in A.D. 558.

Structural Loadings

The first step for determining the dead-weight *gravity loadings* acting within a structure is to calculate the volumes of material and the locations of the centers of gravity of the individual building elements—usually from detailed drawings of the building, often supplemented by on-site measurements. The magnitudes of the loadings are then found by multiplying the volumes by a standard unit weight for the particular material; for example, the normal unit weight (indicated by γ) of construction stone is 2,400 kg/m^3 (150 lb/ft^3).

To estimate the *wind load* on a tall building, one must first consult local meteorological records for the general wind speeds and directions over extended periods of time, as well as theoretical wind-velocity profiles (velocity variation according to height above ground level) for the particular terrain of the building site. Wind-velocity data over long periods of time, even as long as a century, can usually be obtained from governmental meteorological sources. The profile of wind velocity shown in figure 2.3, over level terrain, is for "surface roughness" assumed to correspond to a pre-industrial city. Maximum winds normally occur over a fairly wide azimuth, so the full wind loadings are considered to act in their most critical direction—usually transverse to a building's longitudinal axis. Wind-pressure distributions (and suction on the leeward side of a building) are then calculated from these data, and from wind-tunnel test data for the particular configuration of the building, by means of the equation

$$p = \tfrac{1}{2}\rho \times V^2 \times C \times G$$

where p is the wind pressure; ρ is the mass density of air, taken as 0.135 kg-sec^2/m^4 (0.00256 lb-sec^2/ft^4); V is the wind velocity; C is a dimensionless coefficient related to building form; and G is a gust factor to account for the dynamic action of impinging air.

The variation of the *pressure coefficient* C across both windward and leeward surfaces is established from wind-tunnel tests of primary building forms placed in constant-velocity fields and in fields reflecting the variations in wind velocity that accompany changes in building height to produce flow reversals and eddy formations not present in a constant-velocity field.[10] For the calculation of windward pressure and leeward suction on the walls of a typical large Gothic church, the positive values of C range from 0.5 to 0.9, and the negative (suction) values from −0.4 to −0.7.[11]

The *gust factor* G—which takes into account the height-to-width aspect ratio, the natural frequency and damping of the structure, the roughness of the background terrain, and gust energy based on wind wave distributions—offers a relatively simple way to measure the dynamic influence of the wind. For the major Gothic buildings, a constant gust factor can be taken as 2.3, which accounts for the maximum possible dynamic effect of wind on this type of building.[12] From such a calculation, and from the surface "sail areas" on which the wind pressure acts, the maximum total lateral loading from wind pressure and suction on a typical bay in

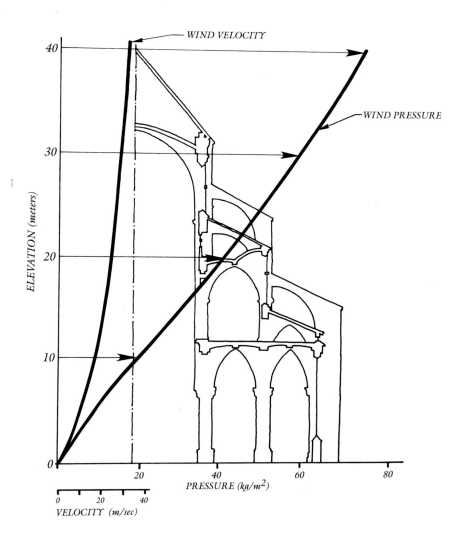

2.3

Wind velocity profile and parametric
wind pressure variation (with C = 1.0)
versus building height, based on modern
data from Paris and the terrain of a
medieval city.

the original nave of the cathedral of Notre-Dame de Paris (illustrated in figure 2.4) was estimated to be 52,000 kg (117,000 lb). For comparison, the total dead weight of each bay, exclusive of the foundations, was computed to be 2.1 million kg (4.6 million lb).[13]

Scaling

Dimensional analysis, developed as an offshoot of theoretical physics, provides a powerful tool for designing experiments with small-scale models and for scaling the behavior of a model to the full-scale prototype. Scaling theory, based on dimensional analysis, indicates that if the dimensions of the model are kept in scale with those of the prototype, if the distribution of loadings is the same in the model as in the prototype, and if the materials of the model behave as those in the prototype, then there exists a set of *dimensionless* parametric terms (ratios having no dimensions) that relate the dimensions of the structure and the loadings acting on it to the resulting internal forces, deformations, and stresses, which apply equally to both the model and the prototype.[14] For instance, a dimensionless ratio relating stress f at any point in a building to the total loading acting on the building Q and its overall length L is

$$f \times \frac{L^2}{Q}$$

Since this dimensionless ratio applies to both the full-scale prototype (represented by the subscript p) and the scale model (represented by the subscript m), we have

$$f_p \times \frac{L_p^2}{Q_p} = f_m \times \frac{L_m^2}{Q_m}$$

This identity yields

$$f_p = f_m \times \frac{(L_m/L_p)^2}{Q_m/Q_p}$$

where L_m/L_p is the dimensional-scale factor (model to prototype) and Q_m/Q_p is the load-scale factor (model to prototype). The equation signifies that the stress acting at any point in the prototype building structure can be determined by multiplying the stress found at a corresponding point in a similar model by the square of the dimensional-scale factor and then dividing the product by the load-scale factor.

Dimensional analysis can also be used to answer more general queries, such as the question raised by Galileo's proposition that attention to geometry alone in design is not sufficient to ensure successful structure. This is illustrated by a comparison of the stresses caused by self-weight in two buildings having the same form and constructed of the same materials but at different scales. A dimensionless ratio relating stress f at any point in a building to its dead-weight loading, which in turn is a function of the average density of the construction materials γ and its overall length L, is

$$\frac{f}{\gamma} \times L$$

Since this dimensionless ratio applies to a building of any scale, we have (where subscript ℓ indicates large scale and subscript s small scale)

$$\left(\frac{f}{\gamma} \times L\right)_\ell = \left(\frac{f}{\gamma} \times L\right)_s$$

If the same materials are used in both buildings ($\gamma_\ell = \gamma_s$), this identity yields

$$f_\ell = f_s \times \frac{L_\ell}{L_s}$$

which reveals that the stresses due to self-weight are proportional to the relative size of a building (L_ℓ/L_s), with the larger buildings subject to the higher stresses. This is the case because the volume, and hence the dead-weight loading, increases with the cube of a building's scale, while the areas of the supporting structures within the building increase only as the square of its scale.[15] Moreover, because of the generality of the dimensional analysis method, this inference applies to *all* types of stress, including the shear and bending stresses caused by shear forces and bending moments that may be acting within the building structure.

Structural Modeling

Modern engineers have developed analytical solutions for many types of structural configurations, but these are usually limited to those with well-defined regular geometries and loadings. Modeling is used to solve for deformations and for force and stress distributions within more intricate structures. One approach uses *physical modeling*, in which measurements are taken from a small-scale model and scaled up to the full-scale prototype as discussed above. A second approach uses *numerical modeling*, in which the abstracted material properties, geometry, and loading of the structure are programmed into a computer and used to produce the needed information directly.

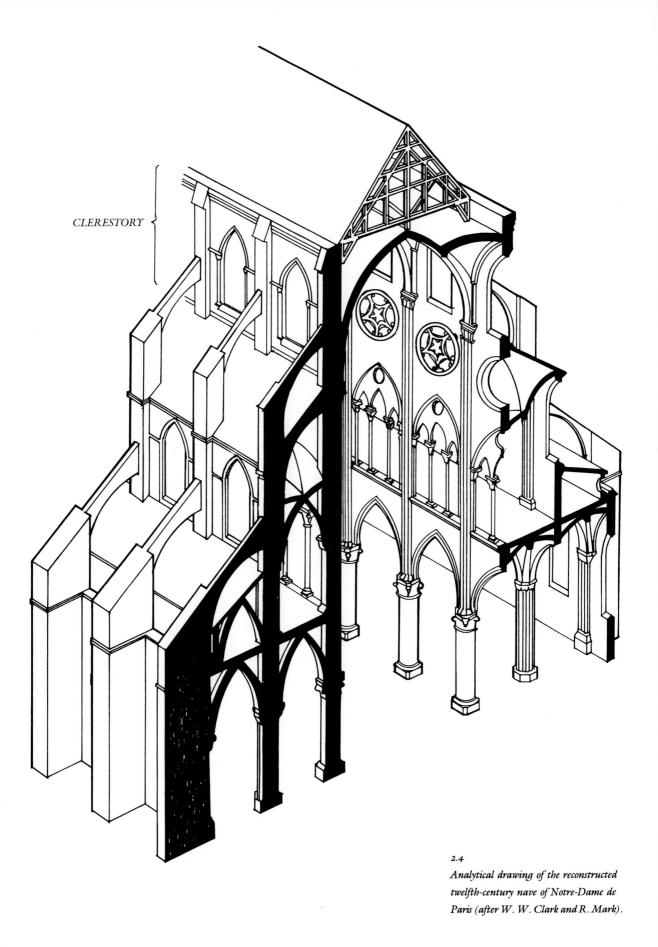

2.4

Analytical drawing of the reconstructed
twelfth-century nave of Notre-Dame de
Paris (after W. W. Clark and R. Mark).

In modeling a building to determine how forces are distributed within its structure, the actual structural configuration is first abstracted to its most basic form in order to simplify the analysis as much as possible. Analysis of the long straight portions of Gothic churches, for example, is facilitated by their repeating modular bay design (as illustrated in figure 2.4). Such buildings can be considered to be supported by a series of parallel, transverse "frames" consisting of the principal load-bearing structural elements: piers, buttresses, lateral walls, and ribbed vaults. These "frames," representative of the critical supporting structure within the building, are reproduced in the model.

Research at Princeton University during the 1960s demonstrated that tests of small-scale plastic models could be used to predict internal forces within complex reinforced-concrete structures subjected to normal in-service loadings, even though concrete is notoriously inelastic, compositionally nonhomogeneous, and subject to tensile micro-cracking.[16] It was this experience with concrete structures that led to the idea that masonry buildings might also be amenable to investigation using small-scale models, but only if the masonry prototype, like the model, acted essentially as a monolith. This holds true if all the individual stones within the masonry are pressed against adjacent stones by compressive forces set up in the interior of the structure in response to environmental loadings. In fact, the assumption also coincides with criteria for successful masonry performance, because (as explained above) mortar tensile strengths are usually so low that structural continuity cannot be maintained in the masonry if any appreciable tension is present. The presumption that all the masonry within the structure acts in compression, however, must still be confirmed by the results of the model test. If extensive regions of tension are found, the model may be altered by slitting it to represent the effects of cracking.

Another assumption is that gravity begins to act only after construction is completed. This is true with structures such as arches or vaulting, which are usually assembled on rigid centering and hence are not subject to dead-weight loadings until the centering has been removed. After very long periods of time, the constant dead-weight loadings can produce unrecoverable viscous flow (creep) in the masonry; wind loadings, which are of variable magnitude and which come from every quarter, cannot cause a similar effect. In any event, if the basic support and form of a

*Computer-drawn perspective of a finite-
element model of quadripartite vaulting.*

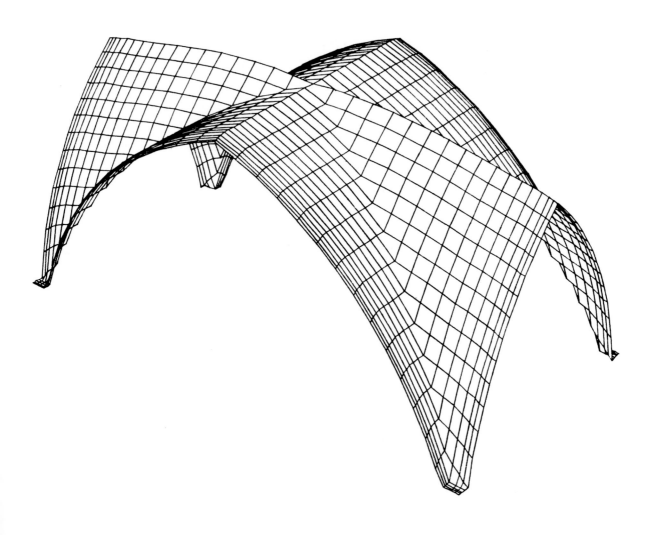

structure remain unchanged with time, the distribution of internal forces will be little altered from the initial elastic pattern.[17]

Numerical modeling involves an approach similar to that used for a physical model. The model's form, however, is now described by a series of coordinates taken at intervals on the structure's surface. In *finite-element* modeling, these coordinates define a mesh that becomes the geometric model for the computer (see figure 2.5). A series of equations related to the loading conditions and to the properties of the prototype materials are then used to calculate the displacement at each point in the mesh in order to obtain the displacement pattern for the entire structure. That pattern then gives, through equations of elasticity, the same type of information about the overall distribution of structural forces that is obtained by testing a physical model.[18]

A recent study of the roof of Westminster Hall in London serves to demonstrate the application of combined physical and numerical modeling as well as many of the structural concepts discussed above. The hammer-beam roof of the hall—a product of the English Late Gothic tradition of monumental carpentry, designed and executed by Richard II's "chief carpenter" Hugh Herland between 1393 and 1397—spans almost 21 m (68 ft), and is by far the largest roof of its type ever constructed.[19]

Although there had been much commentary on the design of the hall's roof framing, uncertainty about the functioning of its structural elements remained unresolved.[20] The main questions about its structure were these:

• Is the frame supported primarily at the top of the masonry wall, or low down on the wall at the level of the corbel?
• Does the hammer beam (which for both iconographic and decorative purposes is carved as an heraldic angel) play any real structural role in supporting the roof? If it does, was that role understood in Herland's original design?
• Do the joint intersections permit continuity of individual members, particularly in the great arch?

To resolve these questions, we constructed a 1:10-scale timber model conforming to Herland's framing (as it was constructed in 1395), using all the available archaeological information (including details of the joints).[21] The model was made from well-cured American red oak, chosen because of its general resemblance to the English oak used by Herland. The effect of the dead-weight loading on the major purlins of the full-scale frame was simulated

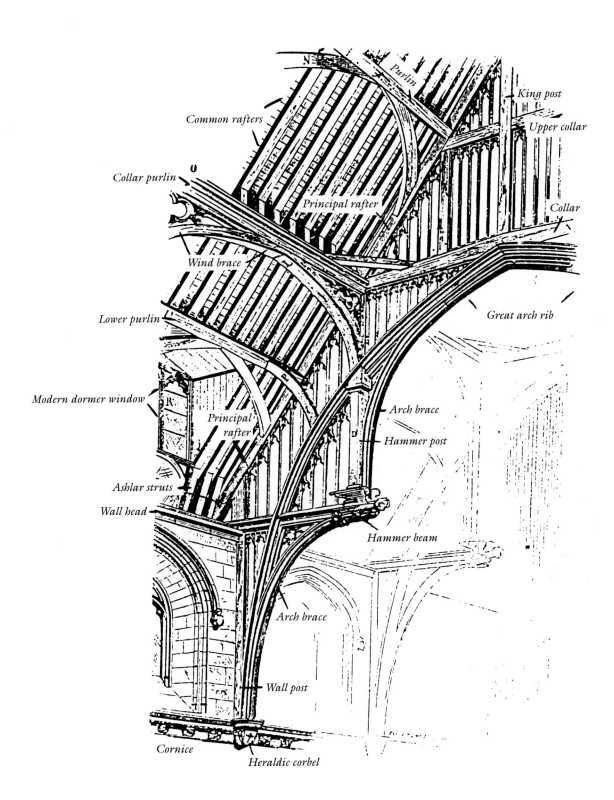

2.6

Framing of Westminster Hall, London (ca. 1400) with timber-roof nomenclature (after Viollet-le-Duc).

Common rafters

Purlin

King post

Upper collar

Collar purlin

Principal rafter

Collar

Wind brace

Great arch rib

Lower purlin

Modern dormer window

Principal rafter

Arch brace

Hammer post

Ashlar struts

Wall head

Hammer beam

Arch brace

Wall post

Cornice

Heraldic corbel

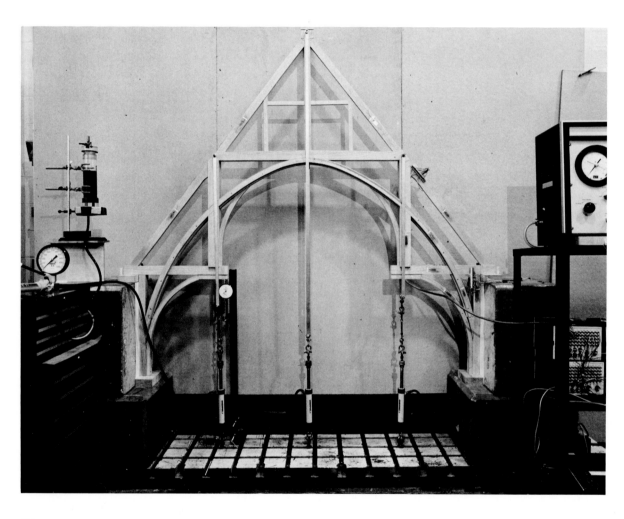

2.7

1:10-scale timber model of the Westminster Hall roof frame. Note hydraulic loading system, dial indicator for deflection measurements, strain gauges, and removable blocks under supports. (photo: J. W. Williams)

in the model with three hydraulic jacks, which were activated simultaneously by a hand pump. A pressure gauge was used to control the jack loads. And to ensure good correspondence between the behavior of the model and that of the prototype, particularly within the member joints, the magnitudes of the test loadings were chosen so that the model would be subject to the same levels of *strain* as the prototype.

Since low levels of strain in wood can be taken to be linearly proportional to stress, the scaling relationship between model and prototype stress developed in the preceding subsection could be used to specify the model test loading. For strains (and, hence, stresses too) in a model and a prototype of the same material to be equal, this scaling relationship degenerates to

$$Q_m = Q_p \times \left(\frac{L_m}{L_p} \right)^2$$

This indicates that the model loading (Q_m) should be reduced from the prototype loading (Q_p) by the square of the model scale factor (L_m/L_p). For a 1:10-scale model, then, the model loading should be $\frac{1}{100}$ of the prototype loading; in effect, a hydraulic-jack loading of 100 kg (220 lb) represents a load of 10 metric tons (22,000 lb) applied at a purlin in the full-scale structure. A similar reduction in force is experienced by the individual structural members; that is, full-scale-member forces are 100 times the forces acting in the members of the 1:10-scale model.

The instrumentation consisted of machinist's dial indicators (used to measure deflections) and pairs of metal-foil electric-resistance strain gauges (figure 2.8) attached at the center lines of the major members. (The gauges function by indicating a change in electrical resistance as they strain together with the base material.) Through calibration with known loads, strain measurements were used to find the axial forces within the individual members. But because of natural variation in timber properties (as compared with the relative homogeneity of plastics or metals, for which strain gauges are more normally used) and because of the low levels of axial strain in both the full-scale structure and the model, the force determinations from the model tended to be ragged.[22] Hence, readings taken from the timber model were used primarily to determine the *general* behavior of the frame. A more refined numerical (computer) model, in which the support conditions and the member-joint behavior were based on observations of the behavior of the timber model, was then used to obtain the final quantitative force distribution. This numerical model is illustrated in figure 2.9.

2.8
Detail of model of Westminster Hall roof frame showing installation of electric-resistance strain gauges on (from top to bottom) lower principal rafter, segment of great arch, hammer post, hammer beam, and curved brace. (photo: J. W. Williams)

2.9
Numerical model of Westminster Hall roof frame showing applied purlin loadings, support reactions, and member-force distributions (with forces in metric tons).

In addition to the importance of careful construction and instrumentation of the timber model, it was important to simulate the support conditions provided by the masonry wall at different levels. Thus, for testing purposes, the model was mounted on massive concrete blocks, recreating the known rigid-wall support of the prototype. The exterior ends of the hammer beams (on the top of the wall) and the bases of the wall posts (at the level of masonry corbels) were supported on respective pairs of closely fitted, removable wooden blocks (illustrated in figures 2.7 and 2.8). This allowed the model to be easily tested with three different configurations of vertical support relating the roof to the wall: (a) full support at both wall head and corbel, with both blocks in place; (b) support only at the corbel level, with the upper blocks removed; and (c) support only at the wall head, with the lower blocks removed.

Despite the noted difficulties with the strain-gauge data, the timber model displayed good consistency of behavior in deflection and in the distribution of forces, and it served well to demonstrate which of the possible support conditions was in fact originally

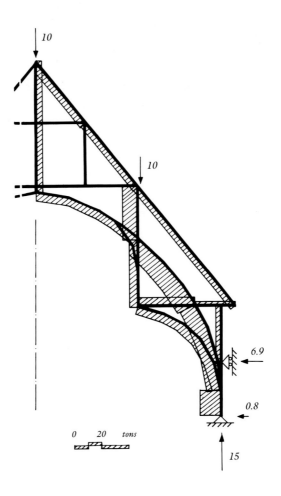

chosen by Herland. The most significant experimental observation was obtained with the model supported in configuration c (with the corbel support removed): Under only a partial loading, the joints of the great arch and the wall posts of the model began to separate. Thus, it became immediately clear that allowing vertical support to the frame only at the top of the wall was structurally untenable. For model configuration a (with vertical support both at the wall head and the corbel) and configuration b (with vertical support only at the corbel), the downward reflections of the inner ends of the hammer beams were essentially the same (0.7 mm) and the outward deflections of the hammer beam ends were of similar magnitude. According to scaling theory, the full-scale frame would have deflected 10 times as much as the model, which is still a very small amount and which indicates that the original roof structure must have been extremely rigid.

For all practical purposes, the *full vertical support* of the roof frame, even when support at the wall head is left in place, is provided by the corbel and the wall post. The member forces illustrated in the computer solution of figure 2.9 are essentially the same for loading conditions a and b. Thus, the major structural issues of the Westminster Hall frame have been resolved on the basis of the "dialogue" between the observable behavior of the timber model and the more refined numerical modeling (both scrutinized against available archaeological information). The frame is actually supported at the level of the masonry corbel *about halfway down from the top of the wall*, mainly by the combined action of the heavy hammer posts (which take the load from the purlin) and the great arch (which acts as a *continuous* member to convey much of the vertical dead load and the horizontal thrust received from the hammer posts and hammer beams, respectively).

The angel hammer beams are important functional members. They were found to carry appreciable *tension*, in contrast to all the other major elements of the frame acting in compression, and thus to restrain the outward thrust of the rafters. These findings indicate that Herland intended to bring the reactions of this immense roof lower down on the thick Norman walls, where they are better able to resist horizontal forces. The effect is the same as lowering the bending moment "arm" for a buttress (that is, reducing the distance y illustrated in figure 2.1b) and, in so doing, lowering the bending moment and the possibility of tensile cracking in the supporting wall.

Human response to light is highly subjective. For many pre-modern commentators, it had even a metaphysical dimension.[23] In parallel with sound's attributes of pitch, loudness, and unmeasurable "quality," the sensation of light is associated with *brightness, hue,* and *saturation.*[24] Whereas hue and saturation refer to color, brightness—which is quantified in terms of surface *illuminance* (rather than *intensity,* a term that should be used only to define the emission of a light source)—can be readily measured with a photocell. Yet the human eye readily adapts to wide variations in light levels; however, it has difficulty discerning patterns in contrasting light, such as in a relatively dark region of an otherwise bright space.[25] Hence, any attempt to quantify levels of illumination within historic buildings needs to be accompanied by judicious interpretation. But by taking advantage of some simple physical concepts used in designing modern artificial lighting, we can better understand the early designers' intentions for using natural light.

Light-source intensity has long been defined in units of candlepower. The term is still employed for many lighting standards, despite the substitution for the "standard candle" (based on a no. 6 sperm-oil candle burning at a definite rate) of a "new standard" consisting of one square centimeter of "fused thorium oxide at the temperature of freezing platinum" and having 60 times the intensity of the old standard candle.

The light received from a standard candle by one square unit of the surface of a one-unit-radius sphere (the unit may be either a meter or a foot; the same total amount of light energy will be received by both unit-area surfaces) is defined as one *lumen* (see figure 2.10). And since the entire area of a one-unit-radius sphere is $4\pi = 12.6$ square units, the amount of light emitted by a standard candle is 12.6 lumens. Assuming no losses in transmission (as would occur in a smoke-filled space), a sphere having a radius of two units will receive the same total amount of light as the first sphere; but since the area of the second sphere is 4 times as great, each unit area receives but $\frac{1}{4}$ the illumination. This phenomenon is described by the *law of inverse squares:*

$$B = I/S^2$$

where B is the surface illuminance (in foot-candles or in lumens per unit area), I is the intensity of the light source (in standard candles or in lumens), and S is the distance from the source to the lighted surface (the "*light-path length,*" in feet or meters).

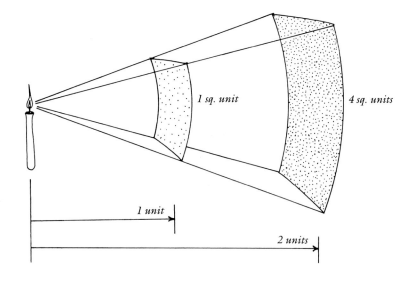

1 sq. unit

4 sq. units

1 unit

2 units

For buildings that depend on natural light, the internal light
sources are openings in the walls or in the roof, usually sky-lit
rather than lit by direct sun, with the source intensity dependent
upon myriad factors such as the intensity of exterior light at different times of the day, possible interference by other structures,
the orientation of the opening relative to sources of exterior light,
and the transmission permitted by window glass (a particularly
important factor when stained glass is fitted). The level of illuminance at any point on a surface within the buildings's interior is
then related to the orientation of the light paths to the point, relative to the axis of the source-light openings, as well as to the
length of the light paths. For example, in figure 2.11, where the
light path from a wall opening to a point on the floor is aligned
at 45° with respect to the axis of the opening, the window would
appear foreshortened to an observer on the floor; hence, the
source light available to illuminate the surface would be a function
of the window's height times cosine 45° (0.707), or but 71 percent
of the total available source light. Other light will of course reflect
off the interior walls, but such reflection from normally rough surfaces is scattered in all directions, reducing the effective light
transmission.

The ancient Pantheon in Rome provides a striking example
of the efficient lighting of a large interior space. Light enters from
a single opening (the oculus) at the crown of the dome. The area
of the oculus is less than 4 percent of the area of the building's
floor. This relatively small opening, however, is oriented to admit

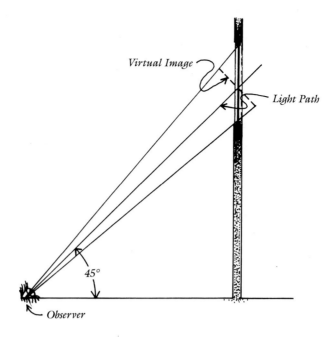

2.12

Section through Pantheon (Rome, ca.
118–128), indicating pattern of light
radiation from central oculus.

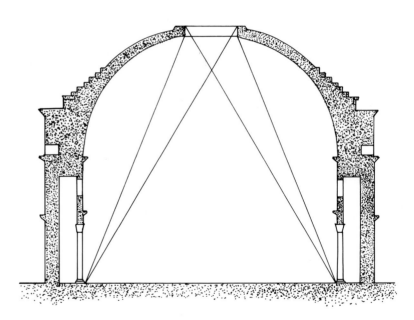

a maximum of light from the brightest area of the sky. No glass is present to reduce transmission, and the orientation of the opening with respect to the temple floor allows close to 100 percent of the radiated source light to reach the floor some 43 meters (143 feet) below. (The cosine of the angle of all the light paths to the floor with respect to the opening axis, as illustrated in figure 2.13, is close to 1.)

Finally, the question discussed at the beginning of this chapter concerning the effect of a change in building scale on natural-light interior illumination can be addressed by applying principles of dimensional analysis. If the intensity of a broad, *diffuse* light source is expressed in lumens per unit area of source opening (Φ), a dimensionless ratio relating surface illuminance (B) to available-source light intensity is B/Φ. As Φ is given in the same units as brightness (lumens per unit area), no additional length term is needed. And since this dimensionless ratio applies to buildings of any scale, we have (with subscript ℓ for large scale and s for small scale)

$$(B/\Phi)_\ell = (B/\Phi)_s$$

Assuming the same source intensity for both buildings ($\Phi_\ell = \Phi_s$), this identity yields $B_\ell = B_s$. Hence, a larger building will receive the same surface illuminance as a smaller, similar building. The basis of this simple relationship is clarified by the fact that whereas the longer light paths within a larger building reduce surface illuminance by an inverse-square relationship, the size of the window openings (and hence the total amount of available natural light) increases with the square of the building's scale. Thus, the two effects cancel each other. With the notable exception of the classical Greek temple, it is actually quite rare to find a larger building scaled up in all its dimensions from a smaller-scale prototype. As will be shown in chapter 4 regarding the development of the Gothic cathedral, the medieval designers did indeed experiment with building sections in order to maintain adequate levels of interior light.

Although the approaches described in this chapter have not often been applied to the study of historic architecture, the accounts that follow demonstrate the power of the methodology, particularly when it is used in conjunction with other available documentation and/or archaeology.

Upper dome and oculus of the Pantheon.
The sun acts as the "point" source of the
illuminated spot on the inner wall;
hence, spot illuminance is essentially un-
diminished by the effect of the distance
from the oculus to the wall.

3

Reinterpreting Ancient Roman Structure

Extensive ruins throughout Europe, the Near East, and North Africa testify to the vast scale of the many public buildings and works of Imperial Rome—amphitheaters, baths, markets, temples, bridges, and aqueducts. Yet contemporaneous documents giving details of the design or descriptions of the construction of those works are almost nonexistent. The most complete text that has come down to us is the work of the Roman architect and military engineer Vitruvius, who finished *The Ten Books of Architecture* just at the beginning of the Imperial era, shortly before the birth of Christ—well before the onset of the major building activity.[1] Hence, most of the historical evidence must come from the buildings themselves. A number of these, including the Roman Colosseum and the Large Baths of Hadrian's Villa at Tivoli, have survived sufficiently intact to indicate their original form and construction. And by a stroke of unusual good luck (because it was consecrated as a church five centuries after its construction), one of the largest and most influential buildings of the era, the Roman Pantheon, has been preserved almost perfectly.[2]

Much of the material in this chapter was derived from the following works: R. Mark and Paul Hutchinson, "On the Structure of the Roman Pantheon," *Art Bulletin* 68 (March 1986): 22–34; R. Mark, "Reinterpreting Ancient Roman Structure," *American Scientist* 75 (March-April 1987): 142–151; R. Mark and Anne Westagard, "The First Dome of the Hagia Sophia: Myth vs. Technology," in *Domes from Antiquity to the Present*, Proceedings of the 1988 International Symposium of the IASS, ed. I. Mungan (Mimar Sinan Üniversitesi, 1988), pp. 163–172. For wider historical background on the architecture of the era, see J. B. Ward-Perkins, *Roman Imperial Architecture* (Penguin, 1981).

3.1

Aqueduct, Segovia, Spain, first century A.D. Detail of upper arcade.

3.2

Colosseum, Rome, inaugurated 80 A.D.

The circular-domed Pantheon (figure 3.4), constructed ca. A.D. 118–128 by the Emperor Hadrian, replaced a rectangular-plan temple (similar in form to a classical Greek temple) that had been destroyed by fire. The inscription from the earlier temple— M·AGRIPPA·L·F·COS·TERTIVM·FECIT (Marcus Agrippa, the son of Lucius, three times consul, built this)—is still displayed on the entrance portico, and this caused much confusion about the actual construction dates. The enigma was solved only in our own time when brickyard stamps found on bricks used in the original wall facing were securely dated.[3] The new temple appears to have been dedicated to all the gods; however, it is known that Hadrian also held judicial court in the Rotunda.

The clear span of the Pantheon, 43.3 m (143 ft), is far greater than that of any known earlier domed building. In fact, this span remained unmatched for well over a millennium, until the completion in 1446 of Brunelleschi's dome for the cathedral of Florence; and it was not matched again until 1590, with the erection of Michelangelo's dome for St. Peter's. Since the spans of these two largest Renaissance domes are within one meter of that of the Pantheon, the Pantheon's dome was likely used by the designers of those buildings as the model to determine the upper limit for masonry dome construction (see chapter 5). Moreover, it was not until the middle of the nineteenth century that the span of the Pantheon was substantially surpassed, with the introduction of metal-framed structures for long-span railroad sheds and exhibition halls. The Galerie des Machines, constructed together with the Eiffel Tower for the Paris Exposition in 1889, spanned 111 m (364 ft). In this century the limits have been further extended by thin reinforced-concrete roof shells; the record span for a thin shell—that of the roof of the C.N.I.T. Exhibition Hall, built in Paris in 1958—is 219 m (718 ft).[4]

The Pantheon also marks the zenith of the reign of the Roman emperors, which began in 27 B.C. with the granting of the title of Augustus to Caesar Octavian. An era of unusual internal stability followed, accompanied by foreign conquest and expansion, unprecedented trade, and the flow of such great wealth into the capital that it would completely alter Rome's topography. With the construction under imperial aegis of many lavish, large-scale buildings, great numbers of skilled craftsmen were imported, including marble workers from Greece. Whole "armies" of slave laborers from the conquered territories were pressed into work on

3.3
Hadrian's Villa, Tivoli, Large Baths,
ca. 120.

3.4
Dome of the Pantheon in the modern
Roman cityscape. (photo: S. Ćurčić)

3.5

Interior of the Pantheon.

the construction. According to his contemporary Suetonius, Augustus boasted that he "found Rome a city of brick and left it a city of marble."[5]

This frenetic building activity, which continued with hardly a pause, was facilitated at the end of the first century A.D. by the general Roman adoption of structural concrete, which had previously been used only for utilitarian structures, such as the terrace constructed early in the first century B.C. to support a now-lost temple of cut stone at Terracina on the Via Appia. Concrete was now to be used even for major monuments, usually as a core between brick forms which then became the permanent exterior facing of the building (a type of construction known as *opus testaceum*).

Modern historians have continued to attach much significance to this change in ancient building materials, as is illustrated by a recent comment about the famed Roman Colosseum, which was erected only a half-century before the Pantheon. Intended to hold some 50,000 spectators and built on a framework of squared blocks of travertine limestone which constitutes its load-bearing skeleton, this great amphitheater has been described by the archaeologist John Ward-Perkins as "a building of not any great originality," as "conservative in its structural methods and choice of materials as it was in design," and as representing "a strain in Roman architecture that was shortly to be swept away by new techniques and new aspirations."[6] Such remarks about a building almost as influential in the history of architecture as the Pantheon are based on what historians perceive to have been a "Roman architectural revolution"—a revolution brought to fruition even as the Colosseum was under construction with the transition from conventional masonry structures of brick or solid stone to domed and vaulted buildings using cast "monolithic" concrete for load-bearing structure. The way now seemed open for a whole new genre of large-scale architecture which could be readily cast in curvilinear form. And the building most generally taken to represent the culmination of this "revolution" is the Roman Pantheon, with its massive, brick-faced concrete walls and its great bronze-covered concrete dome. (The bronze covering, because of its value, was removed and replaced by a lead covering in the early seventeenth century; the present-day roof is shown in figure 3.7.)

Roman concrete, as discussed in chapter 2, is similar to modern Portland cement in having hydraulic properties and good strength—perhaps as high as 200 kg/cm^2 (2,800 psi) in compression and 10–20 kg/cm^2 (140–280 psi) in tension. Yet Roman and modern concrete construction differ in two vital details. First, the

3.7
Roof of Pantheon, with lead covering, step rings, and the stairs leading to oculus.

mix consistency of modern concrete is fluid and homogeneous, allowing it to be poured into forms; in Roman practice, concrete was hand-layered together with chunks of aggregate, often consisting of rubble from earlier buildings.[7] Second, the use of integral reinforcing steel gives modern concrete assemblies excellent tensile capacity, whereas Roman concrete could depend only upon the tensile strength of the cement bond to resist tension.

Nevertheless, it has usually been assumed that Roman concrete structures behaved in the same general manner as modern structures of reinforced concrete. In fact, historians have argued that once the Romans developed a concrete that could presumably stand as a monolithic unit, there was little but tradition to limit new architectural forms. In this vein, the structure of the vast dome of the Pantheon has been likened to that of a monolithic metal pot lid.[8] The concentric stepped rings around the base of the dome, which effectively thicken the shell (as illustrated in figure 3.8) have been interpreted as giant reinforcement hoops that act similarly to the hoops used around a wooden barrel. According to this line of reasoning, the stepped rings serve to reduce the circumferential (or "hoop") tensile stresses caused by the tendency of the base to splay outward under the tremendous dead weight of the great dome. Yet the Roman builders continued to support their domes on massive walls. Were they then merely slaves to tradition, as a number of historians have suggested, or did their own understanding of the structure conflict with this modern interpretation? As in the case of the Westminster Hall roof frame, described in chapter 2, the answer to this query may best be found by structural modeling.

3.8

"Cutaway" illustrating concrete-core construction of the Pantheon.

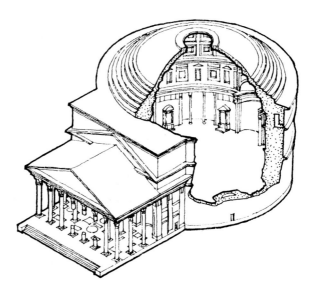

An analysis of the Pantheon was carried out using a three-dimensional, finite-element computer modeling code of the type described in chapter 2, developed by Jean-Herve Prévost at Princeton University.[9] To simplify the modeling, a typical meridional section was specified. Because of the extensive openings in the cylindrical wall—one-fourth of the wall's volume is taken out by statue bays, passageways, and other voids—no typical section actually exists (see figures 3.9 and 3.10). But since our interest is centered on the functioning of the dome and on the conceptional design of the basic structural configuration, we need not deal in detail with the wall.[10] In fact, it is possible to select a solid wall that provides support to the dome similar to that provided by the actual, voided wall. It was determined that a solid cylinder 5.5 m (18 ft) thick provides the same overall structural stiffness as the 6 m (20 ft) thick actual wall; this equivalent wall (shown in figure 3.11) was used throughout the analysis.

A second simplification made for the modeled building section concerns the structural effect of the coffering on the underside of the dome (visible in figure 3.4). The coffers, which form a waffle pattern beginning just above the springing and ending several meters from the oculus, are relatively shallow in comparison with the thickness of the dome, which is taken to be uniform at 1.5 m (4.9 ft) above the stepped rings. A volumetric analysis indicated that less than 5 percent of the weight of the dome is taken out by the coffering. And since it decreases the stiffness of the dome to a similar small degree, the effect of the coffering could be ignored in the model.

Another consideration was the possible interaction of the porch with the rotunda supporting the dome. It was found, though, that the porch is hardly connected to the rotunda and hence plays no role at all. In the model, the base of the rotunda is assumed to be fixed to perfectly rigid foundations, and the dome is assumed to have been erected on rigid timber centering, so that, in effect, the dome forces were "turned on" all at once with the removal of the centering. Most important, for this first series of model tests, the tensile stresses throughout were assumed to be small enough so that the structural fabric of the building would remain integral; in other words, cracking was nowhere permitted.

Dimensions and data on the materials used in the construction were taken from *The Rotunda in Rome*, by Kjeld de Fine

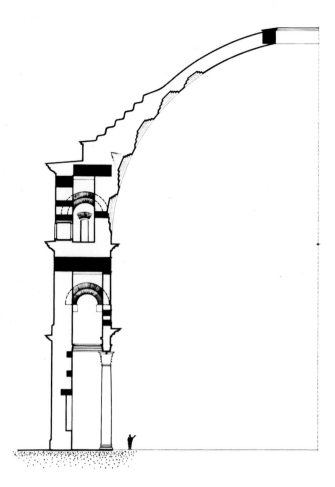

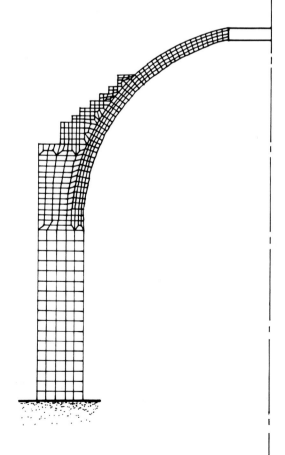

3.10

Meridional section through the Pantheon (after MacDonald).

3.11

Computer-drawn section through finite-element model of the Pantheon.

Licht.[11] The density of the brick-faced concrete used in the cylindrical wall is known to be 1,750 kg/m³ (110 lb/ft³). This value is reduced to 1,600 kg/m³ (100 lb/ft³) in the lower region of the dome, and to 1,350 kg/m³ (85 lb/ft³) in the upper region of the dome (versus the 2,200-kg/m³ [140 lb/ft³] density of the concrete used in the Pantheon's foundations, which is close to the 2,400-kg/m³ [150 lb/ft³] density of standard modern concrete).

Although a hemisphere is not as effective as a pointed dome in reducing bending forces from dead weight, bending throughout the section was found to be relatively low. Indeed, bending forces were low enough so that when their effect was combined with those of the meridional compressive thrusts of the dome, the combined stresses were everywhere compressive in the plane of the section; in other words, no tension was found to be acting along the meridians. Furthermore, the indicated total levels of stress were moderate for this type of construction. The highest value of compressive stress in the dome itself is 2.8 kg/cm² (40 psi), and the maximum compressive stress, in the wall at the level of the footings, is 8.4 kg/cm² (140 psi).

Tension was found, but only acting circumferentially. It is caused by outward deformation of the cylindrical wall at the base of the dome, which must be accompanied by increased circumferential length (as if a rubber band were to be wrapped around the wall and stretched by the wall's outward deformation). This stretching of material in the circumferential, or hoop, direction is accompanied by hoop tensile stress. Yet these stresses are low; the maximum value of "hoop tension," near the top of the outer wall, is 0.6 kg/cm² (9 psi)—well below the nominal tensile strength of even a low-grade concrete.

In addition to the "complete" model described above, a number of models having different geometric and loading modifications were studied. These modifications, which could be made with relative ease using the computer-modeling formulation, provided the basis for a better understanding of the structural behavior of the actual building. It was observed, for example, that the light concrete aggregates used for the construction of the dome are indeed quite effective in reducing stress. If the "heavy" aggregate of the walls had been carried into the full dome, the stresses would have almost doubled. In this light, any effect of the dome's coffering in reducing stress is clearly negligible, both because of its almost insignificant weight reduction and because the coffering does not extend to the central oculus. The coffering, then, is seen to be purely an illusionary device.

A more surprising observation is that the tensile hoop stress was reduced by 20 percent when the stepped rings were removed.[12] Moreover, removal of the rings did not beget bending-tension stress in the plane of the meridional section taken through the dome; thus, the unringed configuration turns out to be more reliable structurally than the actual configuration. Evidently, the rings do not have the salutary effect that has been generally assumed. Although the Roman builder did not possess the analytical tools for making this type of detailed stress evaluation, earlier studies of pre-scientific structural development lead me to believe that the Pantheon's designer may have had sound technical reasons for adopting the stepped rings. Yet the indicated tensile stress levels in both the unringed and the ringed dome configuration, even when raised by a "stress concentration factor" to account for the local effects of the many wall openings (as discussed below), seem to be low enough that no further precautions would have been deemed necessary. Hence, one may well ask why the stepped rings were introduced.

One answer is that the rings were not intended to be structural. They provided only a *constructional* advantage: Vertical formwork for their outer contour facilitated the placing of concrete in regions where the natural extrados of the dome was highly sloped.[13] Yet twentieth-century observations of the fabric of the Pantheon suggest a more compelling explanation. The best of these is a regrettably brief report published in 1934 by the Superintendent of the Monuments of Latium, Alberto Terenzio.[14] Because of the spalling in 1930 of "small fragments" from the dome, scaffolding was erected and used for a systematic inspection. With the removal of plaster, the pattern of meridional cracks illustrated here in figure 3.12 became evident.[15] Terenzio inferred that the problem must have occurred very soon after construction, because some of the bricks used for early crack repairs bore the same stamps as those used in original portions of the building. Their distribution about the dome generally corresponds to openings within the upper cylindrical wall which serve to increase local hoop stresses by a factor of 2 to 3.[16] Fractures caused by hoop tension would therefore be expected to originate there. Yet the predicted levels of hoop stress, which are still an order of magnitude less than the nominal tensile strength of a good-quality cement, would not at first appear to cause such fractures. This question is dealt with below; for now it is sufficient to note from Terenzio's

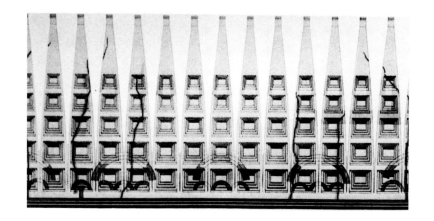

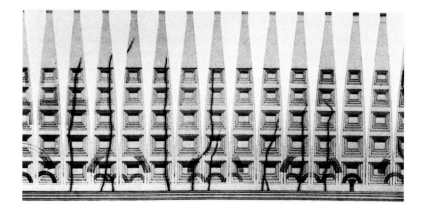

findings that the uncracked models already considered may not best represent the actual structure of the Pantheon, even at the time of its construction.

To account for the observed behavior, a second modeling series was based on an assumption consistent with modern engineering design theory: that the unreinforced Roman concrete could withstand no tensile stresses at all. The model simulation in this case is more complex than for the first test series, because the computer must follow the effect of propagating cracks. The analysis begins with a whole model (as in the first tests), simulates cracks where tension is found, and creates a second, partially cracked model. This second model is then reanalyzed for tension; cracks are propagated through the tension field, and a third model with longer cracks is produced—a process repeated over and over again by the computer and stopped only when the propagation of the cracks becomes insignificant.

These tests indicated extensive meridional cracking of the dome and the supporting wall, which substantially changed the behavior of the dome from that exhibited by the first series of models. A three-dimensional, doubly curved dome gains structural advantage from the interplay between meridional and circumferential (hoop) forces. If the dome is cracked along the meridians, then internal forces in the cracked region are carried only in the meridional direction. Hence, the dome loses much of its three-dimensional advantage; instead of functioning as a "pot lid," it behaves as an array of wedge-shaped arches with a common keystone. And, unlike the generally assumed monolithic shell, these arches require the extremely thick walls of the rotunda below for stability.

The bending of the dome along the meridians was more than twice that found in the corresponding uncracked model configurations. Indeed, the bending was now substantial enough so that the tensile stresses accompanying it (as described in chapter 2) were larger than the compressive stresses arising from the meridional compressive thrusts of the dome. Hence, the combined effect of both forces now resulted in tensile stress in the plane of the dome section. With the step rings omitted, tensile stress was appreciable and covered a large area of the dome extrados. The stress reached a peak of 1.3 kg/cm^2 (18 psi) where the dome joins the raised outer wall. With a model representing the full configuration of the Pantheon, including the step rings, only highly localized tension was observed (at the inner corners of several of the step rings). Since these small regions of tension are in an area that is predominantly compressive, tension cracks would not tend to propagate there and lead to any danger of structural failure. The step rings thus make an obvious and quite possibly crucial difference in the performance of the cracked-section dome.

The extent of the meridional cracking in the actual dome (as recorded by Terenzio and as illustrated in figure 3.12) agrees remarkably well with the simulated cracking in the full model. The documented cracks continue up into the dome to an average of 57° above a horizontal equatorial plane passing through the dome base. The cracking indicated by the model reaches 54° above the equatorial plane of the dome. Above the cracked region, the crown of the dome (including the boundary of the oculus) is entirely in compression, with only moderate levels of stress.

Below the dome, hoop tension in the rotunda wall would be expected to produce vertical cracks. Terenzio does not the illustrate cracks in the wall as he does for the dome, but he does refer to them (see note 15); and I have also observed vertical cracks in the outer wall of the rotunda. The cracking through the modeled supporting cylinder extends all the way down to 7.6 meters above the rotunda floor. Hence, the upper portion of the modeled wall is no longer acting structurally as a cylinder; rather, it is acting as a circular array of independent piers which, according to the analysis, are more than adequate to support the dome.

The coincidence of the behavior of the cracked model with that of the actual structure of the Pantheon indicates that, for practical purposes, Roman pozzolana concrete, despite its outstanding properties, could not be counted upon to exhibit tensile strength. As was discussed above, this inference is at odds with the position taken on Roman construction by most historians; neither does it agree with some recent observations by technical commentators.[17] Moreover, I suspect that it would seem to be at odds with data from tests of the actual concrete used to construct the Pantheon. As had already been noted, the reported maximum stresses due to dead loads are all too low to cause such extensive cracking by themselves. Nevertheless, I inferred that the presence of relatively low tensile stresses over extensive regions of the brittle, unreinforced concrete structure creates conditions especially sensitive to cracking caused by superimposed additional stresses (such as those associated with the curing of newly cast concrete) or by environmentally produced temperature gradients (such as those caused by a sudden temperature drop during a rain shower). Rapid cooling from a "sun shower" wetting the dome surface during an otherwise hot, sunny day could easily induce tensile stresses as high as 15 kg/cm² (210 psi) at the surface of the dome.[18] The cracks caused by the stresses associated with transient conditions then tend to remain open in regions subject to constant dead-weight tension, even after the termination of the transient. In regions of compression, on the other hand, the cracks tend to close, as they apparently have in the upper portion of the dome, near the oculus. As further corroboration, a pattern of cracking only in their lower regions seems to have been a characteristic of many Roman domes—see, for instance, the pattern illustrated in an eighteenth-century drawing by Giambattista Piranesi of the Tempio della Tosse (Temple of Coughs), a relatively small Pantheon-like domed building constructed in the third century at Tivoli (figure 3.13).

From modeling abetted by archaeological observation, then, it appears that Roman builders were well aware of the problem of tensile cracking and took steps to cope with it. Because of the meridional cracking, and the consequent behavior of a large portion of the dome as an array of arches, the structural action of the stepped rings is much like that of a surcharge over the haunch of an arch (as shown in figure 3.1) or over the springing of a barrel vault, where every section along the vault acts as a simple arch. An example of the latter is illustrated in figure 3.14, which shows the remains of a barrel vault at Hadrian's Villa in Tivoli (constructed contemporaneously with the Pantheon).[19] Evidently the stepped rings are the translation of extensive Roman building experience with planar arches to the construction of a dome of unprecedented scale. Our modeling, then, has led to a new view of the influence of the actual structural behavior on the final design of the Pantheon, and for that matter, also to a reinterpretation of the Roman "architectural revolution."

3.13
"Tempio della Tosse," Tivoli: pattern of cracking drawn by G. Piranesi, 1764.

3.14
Barrel Vaulting of the "Teatro Marit-
timo" at Hadrian's Villa, Tivoli, ca.
118–125.

R o m a n
S t r u c t u r a l
D e s i g n

There is no question that, coinciding with the zenith of Imperial Rome's power and wealth, Roman architecture acquired new aspirations and new techniques of construction. Such periods of exceptional commercial and political activity in a civilization are usually symbolized by large-scale building. And the architecture of the Hadrianic era, of which the Pantheon is probably the prime example, was no exception. Yet our study of the structure of the Pantheon calls into question the generally accepted historical assumption that the success of this new architecture was dependent upon the development of a new building technology.

Rome's contribution to monumental architecture derives mainly from the widespread use of the semicircular arch, which allowed large openings in walls for light and access, and the spatial development (as illustrated in figure 3.15) of the arch form into vaulting: barrel vaulting, generated by a lateral translation of the arch (as in figure 3.14); groined vaulting, formed by two intersecting barrel vaults (as in figure 3.16); and hemispherical domes, the semi-circular arch rotated (as in figure 3.5). The apparent plasticity (because one sees only the final rendering, and not the intricate timber formwork needed to create the complex shapes) and the three-dimensional form of many of the concrete structures (e.g., at Hadrian's Villa) is striking indeed. Yet, the basic constructional idea that generated these domes and the vaulting was still that of the planar arch, with its characteristically deep voussoirs, its surcharge over the springing, and its substantial buttressing to resist outward thrusts.

Roman structural development was nowhere near so radical as that of the late nineteenth century, when the introduction of new industrial materials brought forth a true revolution in building design.[20] A far better analogy is to the development, in the late twelfth century, of the High Gothic Cathedral, for which the stage was set by the significant improvement of medieval building techniques during the preceding half-century. A second major factor leading to the technical success of the Gothic was that new buildings, even though they often took what appeared to be unexplored paths, retained many elements from earlier designs (see chapter 4). In this light, there is special significance in the fact that both the semicircular arch and pozzolana cement found major use in Roman substructures and in other utilitarian construction long before they were adopted for monumental architecture. We know, for example, that a masonry-arch bridge with spans as great

3.15
Shell forms generated from semicircular
Roman arch.

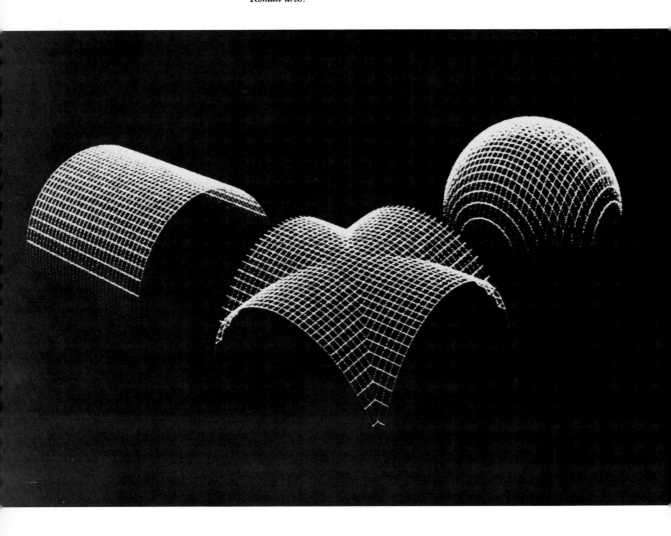

3.16
Groined vaulting of the Baths of Diocletian, Rome, ca. 300. Conversion to the present-day Church of S. Maria Degli Angeli was begun by Michelangelo in 1561.

as 18 m (60 ft), the Pons Mulvius, was placed across the Tiber in Rome as early as 109 B.C., and that between 62 and 21 B.C. it was joined by the Pons Fabricius, which has twin 24-m (80 ft) spans. Furthermore, Vitruvius, writing more than a century before the construction of the Pantheon, discussed in some detail the composition and application of concrete made with pozzolana cement.[21] The decision to begin to employ concrete in large-scale Roman architecture would, then, seem to have been based mainly on economic and constructional rather than purely structural considerations. In view of the availability of building materials, the organization of construction labor, and the evident speed of erection, one cannot doubt that vault construction using cut stone or brick would have been far more costly.[22] But bear in mind that the cost of acquiring large timbers and the need for skilled labor, and hence the great expense of erecting the timber centering used in both types of construction, probably would have been much the same.

Concrete does afford one important *structural* advantage over vault construction of cut stone. It allows, without any special effort, the type of gradation in the weight of materials that was found to be so advantageous in the analysis of the Pantheon. Yet this did not make construction in concrete the only method of choice. Stone and brick continued to be used extensively for monumental construction in the Empire outside of central Italy and, much later, for similarly scaled masonry domes erected over the tall crossing piers of the cathedral of Florence and the basilica of St. Peter in Rome. Indeed, the brick 46 cm (18 in) thick hemispherical dome used by Christopher Wren to enclose the 31-m (101 ft) interior span of the crossing of St. Paul's Cathedral in London provides a valid comparison with the construction of the Pantheon dome. The ratio of thickness to span of Wren's dome, 1:67, if applied to the 43.3-m span of the Pantheon, gives an equivalent thickness of only 65 cm (2.1 ft) instead of the actual 1.5-m thickness of the concrete dome. The outward thrust of a thinner Pantheon dome built of standard brick would thus be similar to that of the actual lightweight concrete dome, and although compressive stresses in a brick dome would be somewhat greater, they could still be easily tolerated.

The building of the Pantheon in a pre-scientific age remains a remarkable achievement. But the technological underpinning of that achievement has been largely misunderstood. Rather than representing a "revolutionary" break with earlier structural tradition, the basic form and support of monumental Roman buildings derived from much previous building experience. The coincidence of the observed cracking within the Pantheon's dome with the model predictions for dome behavior based on concrete having nil tensile strength should put to rest the idea that Roman pozzolana somehow accomplishes feats that no modern designer would expect of unreinforced concrete. Aspects of Roman structural development were no doubt facilitated by the use of pozzolana concrete; but it was not a causal force. Hence, the whole issue of structure and style in the design of ancient large-scale buildings must be reexamined in the context of the actual behavior of the Pantheon dome.

This new point of view bears particularly on the examination of buildings in the far-flung provinces of the empire, where the "Roman architectural revolution" was never fully acknowledged. Indeed, the dark volcanic sands of the type used for manufacturing high-quality pozzolana cements were rarely found outside central Italy, and transportation in bulk (particularly at any distance from the sea) was prohibitively expensive.[23] Moreover, provincial building traditions were not easily set aside. After the beginning of the fourth century, when the political center of the empire was transferred to Constantinople (and along with it the necessary funds for a vastly increased scale of building), local building traditions became all the more important for the course of late Roman architecture.

"Asia Minor," John Ward-Perkins observes, "is a land of fine building stones and marbles, and in Roman times it was still, for the most part, a land of plentiful timber. These were the natural and obvious materials for monumental architecture. There were plenty of cities . . . which remained true to this tradition right down to Byzantine times. As late as the sixth century it was still to dressed stone that the architects of [major buildings, including] the Hagia Sophia in Constantinople, instinctively turned for the piers of their great vaulted monuments."[24] According to Ward-Perkins, even though the indigenous mortar "lacked the strength needed for the creation of vaulting in the fully developed Roman manner," building in Rome—"unquestionably the most progressive architecture of its day"—"was bound to make itself felt all over the Roman world; but its impact could not take the obvious form of direct imitation. What did happen in Asia Minor (to confine the inquiry for the moment to technical problems of vaulting, which was in practice the principal limiting factor) was that a substitute material had to be found, one which might not have all the properties of Roman concrete, but which could be used with a greater freedom than either the dressed stone or the mortared rubble which were its only local alternatives. The material chosen was [fired] brick."[25] Yet brick construction, when used with thick beds of weak mortar, was fraught with problems—as will become evident when we examine that "jewel" of the new imperial capital, the Hagia Sophia, constructed by the Emperor Justinian between A.D. 532 and 537 to replace an earlier church burned down in a riot.

The Hagia Sophia

The creation of the Hagia Sophia, with its vast scale and correspondingly enormous cost, the extraordinary speed of its erection, and its stunning interior space, is unparalleled in pre-modern Western architecture. Since the principal designers, Anthemius of Tralles and Isidorus of Miletus, are known to have been respectively a geometer and a natural scientist, historians of architecture often explain the Hagia Sophia's construction in terms of what might be described as a revolution in technological design.

That perspective is exemplified by Richard Krautheimer's depiction of Anthemius and Isidorus as "what their contemporaries called *mechanopoioi*, grounded in the theory of statics and kinetics and well versed in mathematics . . . that could be applied to the practice of either engineering or building, be it a steam engine . . . or the complex vaulting of H. Sophia. . . . They were, one would like to think, not architects to start with, but they turned into architects when called upon to devise the plans and statics of a building never before considered viable on a large scale."[26]

On the other hand, such an outlook is at odds with the view, commonly held among historians of science, that Galileo's seventeenth-century *Dialogues Concerning Two New Sciences* is the seminal work of analytical structural mechanics.[27] In fact, the development of engineering mechanics to a point where it could begin to treat structural problems as complex as that of a vault is quite recent in origin.[28] Yet if the use of structural theory for the design of the Hagia Sophia's lofty structure is denied, we are still left with the problem of explaining its designers' remarkable technological achievement.

To begin to deal with this problem, it is necessary first to reconstruct the original design, since the building we see today has undergone extensive modification. From surviving sixth-

3.17
*Hagia Sophia, Istanbul, 532–537: south
flank.*

3.18
Hagia Sophia: interior, looking east.

century accounts, it is known that exceedingly large deformations of the main piers supporting the central dome (shown in figure 3.19) disquieted the Hagia Sophia's builders even before the original campaign of construction was completed.[29] The extent of the building's north-south distortion is evident in figure 3.20, which shows the tilt of a pier in the gallery above the main arcade. And in 558 the central dome fell after being subjected to two earthquakes, one in August 553 and one in December 557. A nephew of Isidorus then erected a second dome with a higher profile than its predecessor. The form of the second dome remains basically unchanged despite two more partial collapses, the first after an earthquake in the tenth century and the second following another quake in the fourteenth century. Structural repairs associated with these incidents, as well as other adversities, entailed the placement of much additional buttressing; the building's exterior has thus been greatly altered.[30]

The ribbed central dome, which spans close to 32 m (105 ft), is supported by massive arches, which to the east and the west are partially braced by semidomes (having the same diameter as the central dome) and by huge pendentives having the general form of equilateral triangular segments of a common great sphere whose equator adjoins the lower corners of the pendentive surfaces (see figures 3.21 and 3.22). The pendentive-sphere diameter (D in figure 3.22) is equal to the length of the diagonal across the inside corners of an opposite set of main piers, or 46 m (150 ft).[31] Since Anthemius was a geometer, it would not be at all surprising to find that he intended the interior of the original dome to be formed from the same spherical surface as the pendentives. For such a dome (as illustrated in figure 3.23) the interior radius (that is, the height above the pendentive equatorial plane) would have been 23 m (75 ft). This gives an overall interior height of 50 m (164 ft), about 6 m less than the height of the present dome, which accords with the difference in height between the first and the second dome cited by ancient chroniclers (note 29). And although we have no further direct evidence for a reconstruction of the original dome, some other clues will be provided by a comparison with the great dome of the Pantheon in Rome.

The span of the Pantheon seems to have been unrivaled in late Roman times. It was matched only during the Renaissance, when it appears to have been used as a "model" to determine the

3.19
Hagia Sophia: south interior wall arcade and gallery.

3.20
Hagia Sophia: south gallery pier.

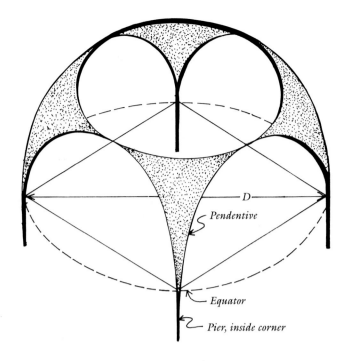

D

Pendentive

Equator

Pier, inside corner

limiting scale of the major domes. However, a comparison (figure 3.24) of the cross-sections of the Pantheon and the Hagia Sophia (taken across the diagonal illustrated in figure 3.22) suggests the need to modify the time scale for this interpretation of the influence of the Pantheon's span. The lower portions of the domes of both buildings are similarly massive (the extent of the solid mass behind the Hagia Sophia's pendentives is indicated in figure 3.25) and provide support to similar, lighter "shells" of fairly uniform thickness above. Both "shells" also subtend angles of close to 90°. Even more surprising, seen in this way, both are of almost the same span, leading to the inference that the limiting scale of the first dome of the Hagia Sophia was determined from the Pantheon in much of the same way as its Renaissance counterparts.

In accordance with Ward-Perkins's concern for the relatively poor strength of local mortars (see note 25), the fact that the Pantheon's dome is constructed of high-grade concrete whereas that of the Hagia Sophia is of brick might seem to rule out any direct structural comparison between these two structures. However, our modeling of the Pantheon revealed that its dome was hardly so monolithic as Ward-Perkins assumed. This inference allows us now to consider the array of windows around the base of the Hagia Sophia dome, which creates the celebrated illusion that

3.23

Reconstruction of a quadrant of the first dome of the Hagia Sophia by H. Prost.

3.24

Comparative sections: Pantheon and H. Sophia (partial section along diagonal).

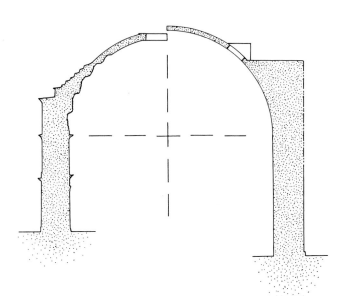

3.25
*Hagia Sophia: upper structure—central
dome, base, and western semidome.*

3.26
Hagia Sophia: dome windows from interior passage.

the dome is suspended above the vast interior space. This configuration was thought to have originated solely for visual effect. Moreover, before we completed our modeling of the Pantheon the placement of these windows in a region of the Hagia Sophia's dome where tensile hoop forces were expected to be critical seemed audacious. But now it is clear that if the base of the dome had been left solid it would have been prone to the same meridional cracking experienced by the Pantheon. The window openings of the Hagia Sophia are thus a prudent expedient to ward off cracking, as well as a dramatic source of light. Although there is no way of knowing with certainty the configuration of the original dome openings, one may hypothesize that it was similar to that of the present windows (see figures 3.21, 3.25, and 3.26). Hence, the openings were likely carried to an angle exceeding 50° above the horizontal equatorial plane. This implies that Anthemius and Isidorus had knowledge of earlier dome fractures, such as those illustrated by Piranesi (figure 3.13). Evidently, the window treatment of the Hagia Sophia derived at least partly from structural concerns and not purely from a stylistic decision.

To try to learn more about the conceptual design of the Hagia Sophia, as well as to discover the cause of the early pier deformation, we analyzed a finite-element model (using the modeling code of note 9) of the first dome idealized as a 75 cm (2.5 ft) thick shell extension of the spherical pendentive surfaces, together with the semidomes and the great supporting arches (see figures 3.23 and 3.27). To represent the likely interaction with the main piers, the model was supported on appropriately stiff elastic supports and, in other tests, on fixed supports with specified displacements. The dimensions of the model were based on the recent survey of Robert L. Van Nice,[32] and, as in the first phase of the Pantheon analysis, the full model was taken to be monolithic. The great main piers of limestone ashlar (visible in figures 3.19 and 3.28) that support the central dome are considerably stronger along their east-west axes than along their north-south axes. In the original design, the piers were braced along the weak (north-south) axes by massive—but, as became evident both from calculation and from archaeological evidence of fracture and distortion, largely ineffective—buttresses composed of brick set in extremely thick beds of mortar, as was discussed in chapter 2.[33] Hence, for purposes of modeling the effect of these "buttresses" was ignored,

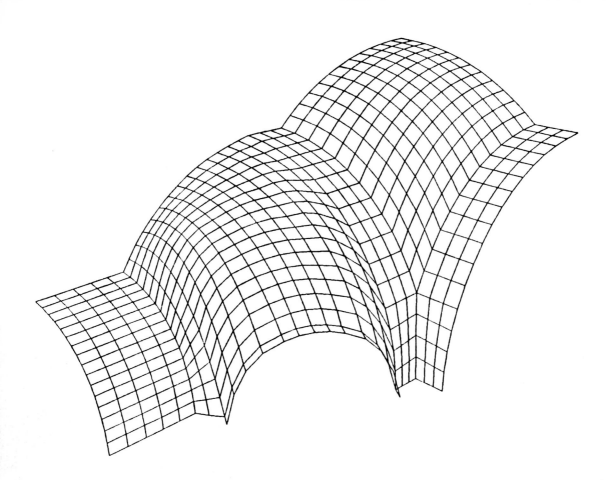

3.27
Finite-element model of the Hagia
Sophia dome, semidomes, and arches.

3.28
Analytical drawing of the Hagia Sophia
structure by H. Prost.

and the stiffness of the modeled piers essentially corresponded to the foreground, "cut-away pier" illustrated in figure 3.28. Although the possibility that the footings might have allowed rotation had been suggested by Emerson and Van Nice (see note 29), the ashlar piers were assumed to be fully fixed at their bases. This assumption seems reasonable, in that the maximum compressive stress at the base of the piers was found to be low relative to the bearing capacity of the solid bedrock below. And the fairly symmetrical deformations of the main piers, reported in note 29, also argues for such fixity.

The results of the model test suggest some further revision of our understanding of the Hagia Sophia's structure. The usual assumption that the semidomes accept a significant portion of the east-west reactions of the main dome, and thereby substantially reduce the concomitant pier forces,[34] is at odds with our findings. The east-west reactions at the top of the main piers were appreciably greater than the outward, north-south reactions: 540,000 kg (1.2 million lb) versus 400,000 kg (900,000 lb). Part of this response is, no doubt, due to the massiveness of the great external arches on the north and south sides of the dome, which generate huge thrusts along their east-west axes and which impinge directly against the piers (figure 3.29). Yet we also found that large, lateral outward displacements of the main piers, which carry the forward edges of the semidomes, appreciably reduced the forces along the boundary of the semidomes with the north-south arches supporting the full dome. Hence, a greater portion of the east-west thrusts from the dome would have to be resisted by the main piers.

Without effective north-south buttressing, the main piers exhibited appreciable tensile stress from bending caused by the outward-acting dome reactions (in a mode similar to that illustrated in figure 2.3b). And although there was no indication of instability or of imminent collapse, the presence of these stresses could help to explain the early, large deformation of the piers.

This modeling of the Hagia Sophia must be considered as only the first phase of a full study. As with the modeling of the Pantheon, a second phase of analysis will have to take cracking of the building fabric into account. Even at this stage of the analysis, however, it is possible to conclude that, like other early designers, Anthemius and Isidorus could use only practical experience in

3.29
*Hagia Sophia: great arch of south wall
under the central dome.*

building as a guide to structural reliability. Geometry did play a
major role in their conceptual design; however, as no less an observer than Galileo also commented,[35] geometry alone can never
ensure structural success. Based on their observations of earlier
construction, Anthemius and Isidorus produced an elegant solution for the first dome of the Hagia Sophia; but the supporting
structure for that dome, particularly the original, weak, thick-
mortared brick buttressing to the north and the south of the piers,
does not seem to have been so well considered.

The Hagia Sophia represents the end of Imperial building
on a grand scale. By the middle of the sixth century the western
portion of the Empire was in decline and (bearing comparison
with events of our own time) the cost of Justinian's military ad-
ventures and vast internal projects, including the building of the
Hagia Sophia, had exhausted the eastern Empire. Yet, as the historian A. A. Vasiliev observed, even though "the majority of Justinian's projects . . . were decidedly out of harmony with the true
interests of the Empire, two of [his] achievements left a deep
mark in the history of human civilization. These are his code of
civil law and the cathedral of St. Sophia."[36]

4

Structural Experimentation in High Gothic Architecture

The prodigious building activity that changed the face of Western Europe and which marks the later Middle Ages as one of the most famous epochs in the history of architecture was accompanied by advances in cloth manufacture and by an enlargement of trade that produced great wealth and led to the growth of cities. It was no accident that the sites of major church construction at the beginning of the thirteenth century—among them Amiens, Arras, Beauvais, Cambrai, and Tournai—were also regions of economic expansion, much of it associated with the cloth trade. Large towns even vied with one another over the heights of their churches, much as Chicago and New York were to do in office towers some seven centuries later. Marked by a refinement of earlier medieval construction techniques and by rapid technological innovation, the rise of Gothic architecture in the twelfth century is seen in this context as a facet of the unprecedented urban growth in the West.

For all of the thousands of monuments that continue to testify to the intensity and scope of Gothic building, there are but a

This chapter was largely derived from the following works: W. W. Clark and R. Mark, "The First Flying Buttresses: A New Reconstruction of the Nave of Notre-Dame de Paris," *Art Bulletin* 67 (March 1984): 47–65; R. Mark and W. W. Clark, "Gothic Structural Experimentation," *Scientific American* 251 (November 1984): 179–185; W. Taylor and R. Mark, "The Technology of Transition: Sexpartite to Quadripartite Vaulting in High Gothic Architecture," *Art Bulletin* 64 (December 1982): 579–587; and R. Mark and Yun-Sheng Huang, "High Gothic Structural Development: The Pinnacles of Reims Cathedral," in *Science and Technology in Medieval Society*, ed. P. A. Long (New York Academy of Sciences, 1985), pp. 125–139. For further information on the modeling of Gothic structure see R. Mark, *Experiments in Gothic Structure* (MIT Press, 1982); for wider historical background see Jean Bony, *French Gothic Architecture of the 12th and 13th Centuries* (University of California Press, 1983).

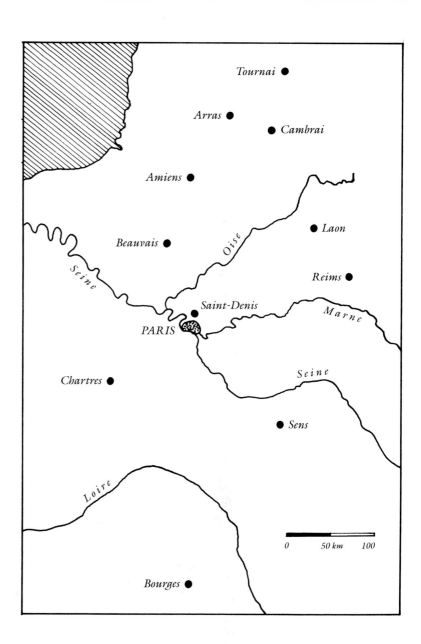

4.1
Map of Northern France showing locations of selected Gothic building sites.

few textual records dating back to before the thirteenth century that document their builders. We know that the great cathedrals were constructed by hired teams of skilled masons and carpenters with supporting staffs and apprentices (who ensured continuity between structural experience and new building). Yet the names of the artisans and artists found in the remaining records (which consist of little more than a few random, appreciative remarks by nonspecialists, most often patrons) make up a remarkably short and inconsistent list. And even those sources give no information about the directives that the patrons must have given to their builders. The classic and uncharacteristically rich example is Abbot

4.3

*Analytical drawing of the nave of
Amiens Cathedral, illustrating Gothic
construction and nomenclature (after
Viollet-le-Duc).*

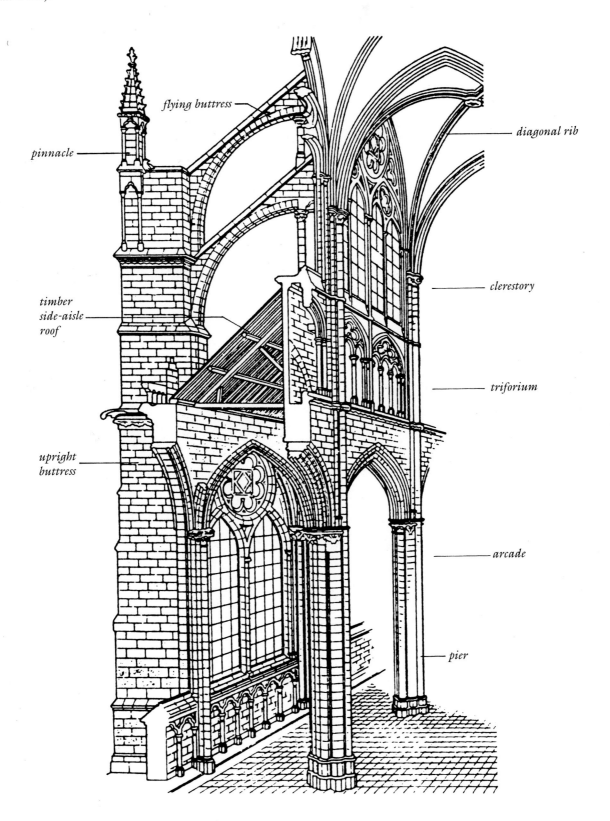

pinnacle

flying buttress

diagonal rib

timber
side-aisle
roof

clerestory

triforium

upright
buttress

arcade

pier

Simulated dead-weight loading being
applied to model of Reims Cathedral
nave structure. (photo: S. Seitz)

4.5
Photoelastic polariscope with model of
Notre-Dame nave structure. (photo:
V. Jansen)

as "stress-freezing." After gradual heating to about 150° Celsius, at which temperature the epoxy changes from its "glassy" room-temperature condition to a "rubbery" state, the weights cause the model to deform. Deformations are locked in as the model is slowly cooled and the epoxy returned to its glassy state. The models are then observed and analyzed with a polarizing-light instrument known as a polariscope. The effects of strain within the model are detected as patterns of light and dark (or of color, when a white-light source is used). These patterns can be read as quantitative contour maps indicating force distributions throughout the model.[4]

Studies combining archaeological observation and engineering modeling have provided new insights into the building methods of the medieval masters. They have suggested, for example, that an earlier building was often used as an approximate "model" to confirm the stability of a new design. Although this practice probably became part of the standard, empirical working procedure, it did not always ensure success. An important instance where building experience may have been inadequate for predicting the behavior of a new design occurred in the planning of what now appears to be the key building in Gothic structural development: Notre-Dame Cathedral in Paris (figure 4.6).

Notre-Dame de Paris

Begun between 1150 and 1155, the choir of the new cathedral of Paris was planned to be the tallest main space in Gothic architecture. With vaulting more than 6 meters (20 feet) higher than that of any of its early Gothic predecessors, Notre-Dame exhibited the largest single-increment height increase for a new church over an earlier building of the era. Even more crucial, it represented the greatest relative change: an increase in comparative height of more than one-fourth over what had been the tallest Gothic churches, the cathedrals of Sens and Laon. Yet despite this dramatic height increase, the structural configuration of the choir of Notre-Dame, whose main altar was dedicated in 1182, repeated the general disposition found in earlier, smaller churches.[5] The outward thrust of the high vaults acting at the base of the clerestory seems to have been resisted mainly by a quadrant arch—a structure similar in form to the later exposed flying buttresses but hidden beneath the sloping gallery roof. The gallery itself—the vaulted second-story space above the ground-level aisle (figures 4.3 and 4.7)—forms a rigid supporting zone that also helps to increase the stability of the wall.

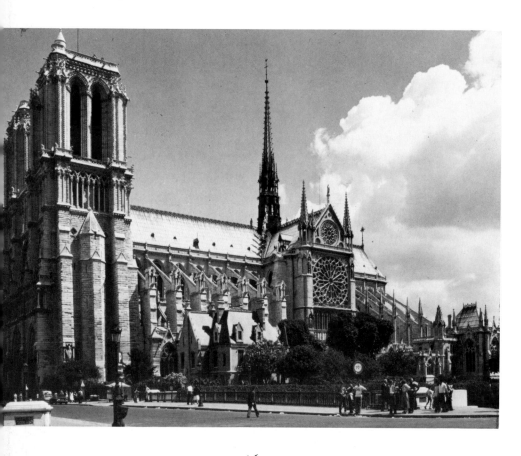

4.6
*Notre-Dame de Paris: View of southwest
flank and transept wall buttress.*

4.7
*Notre-Dame de Paris: interior elevation
of nave and south transept arm. (photo:
J. Herschman)*

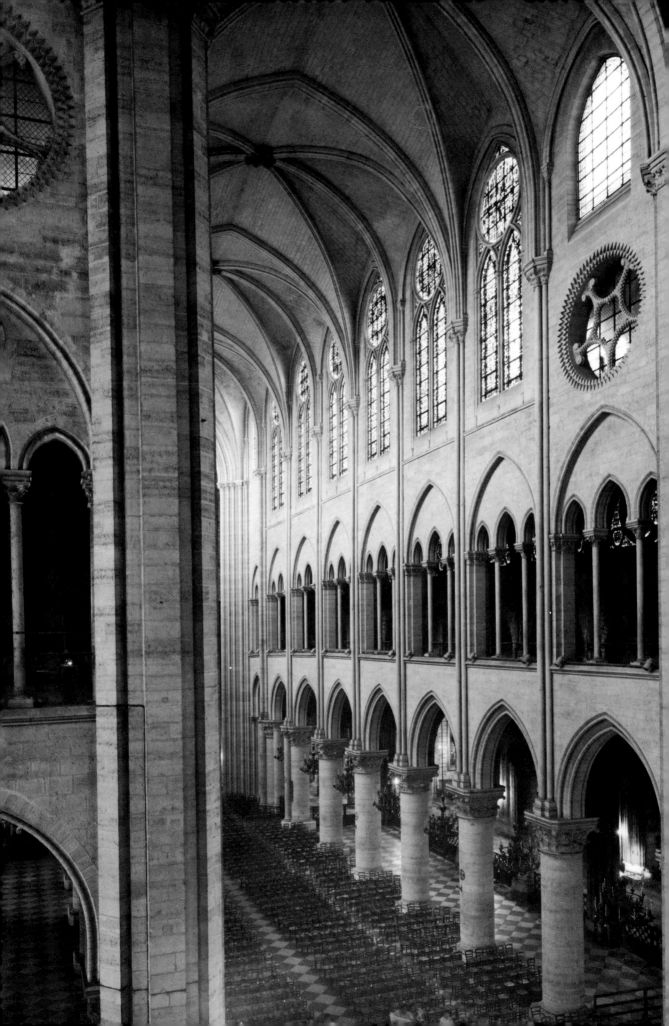

In the nave of Notre-Dame (begun between 1170 and 1175, while the upper works of the giant choir to the east were still under construction), the high vaults were further raised by almost 2 meters, giving a keystone height of 33 m (108 ft) above the floor and increasing the height over that of any earlier Gothic building by one-third (see figure 4.2).[6] The nave is also somewhat wider and more lightly constructed than the choir, and it is likely that the timber roof over the high vaults of the nave was peaked higher than that of the choir, giving the nave an appreciably higher profile overall. Concealed quadrant arches were evidently considered insufficient to support this taller clerestory and raised roof. And the need for adequate bracing was made all the more critical by a new environmental realm singularly associated with tall buildings. At higher elevations above ground level, wind speeds are significantly greater; and since wind pressures are proportional to the square of the wind speeds (as described in chapter 2), experience with lower churches, which also present smaller "sail areas" to the wind, would not have prepared the builders of Notre-Dame to cope with this new design problem. Moreover, the Paris builders seem to have been equally unprepared for the decrease in the amount of light reaching the floor of the choir, another result of this new experiment with height.[7] Concern for interior light no doubt brought about the ramping up of the gallery vaults of the nave, which allowed enlargement of the windows to bring direct lighting to large areas of the floor (figure 4.8). And this, together with concerns for wind loading, seems to have led to the introduction of exposed flying buttresses in the nave of Notre-Dame.

Unfortunately, we have only indirect evidence of the details of this first example of the new structural device. Extensive rebuilding altered the entire buttressing system of the cathedral beginning as early as the 1220s. Another partial reconstruction of the choir apparently took place in the late thirteenth century, but evidence of it disappeared almost completely as a result of the massive rebuilding and restoration carried out in the nineteenth century. Because the original structural system of the nave probably incorporated the earliest examples of flying buttresses, and because we had doubts about the validity of previously proposed reconstructions, William W. Clark and I undertook a new study. This was based largely on an assessment of the archaeological evidence surviving in Notre-Dame itself and in the less-altered little

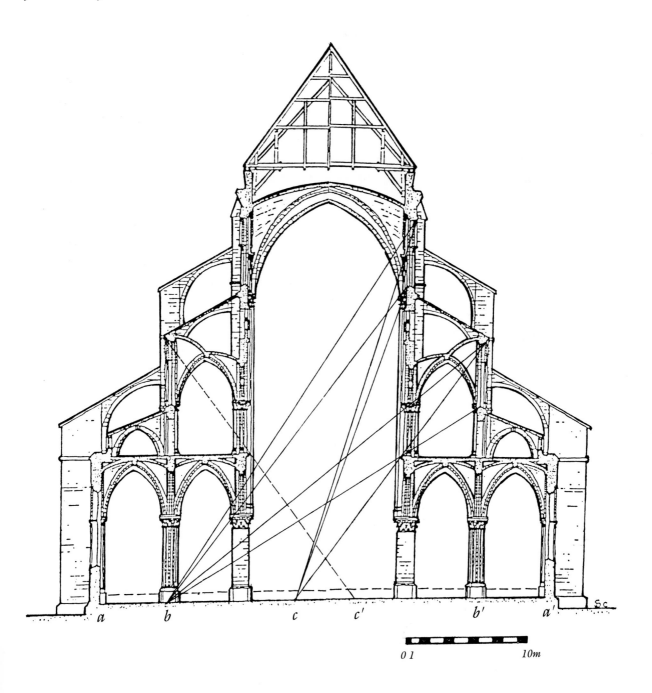

Notre-Dame de Paris: cross-section of reconstructed twelfth-century nave showing
light paths from upper stories. Regions
a–b and a'–b' receive major overhead
lighting from the full gallery windows.
Regions b–c and b'–c' receive oblique
direct light from the clerestory, and only
partial direct light from the gallery windows, because of interference by the gallery floors. Region c–c' receives only
extremely oblique direct overhead light
from the clerestory windows.

01   10m

4.9
Notre-Dame de Paris: original quad-
rant arch in south transept buttress.
(photo: W. W. Clark)

church of Saint-Martin at Champeaux (which was in the posses-
sion of the Bishop of Paris at the time of Notre-Dame's construction), and on documentary evidence preserved in nineteenth-century
pre-restoration drawings and early photographs.[8]

All of this evidence suggested a much simpler configuration
for the first flying buttresses than had been thought. (The cross-
sections of the Notre-Dame nave illustrated in figures 2.2, 4.2, and
4.8 are based on our new reconstruction.) The major archaeological grounds for the reconstruction, still preserved in the building
fabric, can be seen on the back side of the twelfth-century termi-
nal wall buttress on the west side of the south transept (figure
4.9). This region of the cathedral had escaped extensive restoration because of its protected location; yet the evidence remained
undetected because the transept had not had flying buttresses at
least since the thirteenth-century rebuilding. The quadrant arch
embedded in the transept buttress, while never open in the manner of the arch of a true flying buttress, nonetheless reflects the
disposition of the open flyer arches that existed in the adjacent bay
of the nave clerestory.

Historians who previously studied Notre-Dame, and who
focused only on the problem of light, assumed that the changes in
the nave gallery were not sufficient to raise the interior light
level.[9] It was this failure, they argued, that had led to the thirteenth-century decision to enlarge the clerestory windows to their
present size—even though the clerestory enlargement was accompanied by a reduction in the size of the gallery windows (which,
since they were closer to the floor of the church, were in some
ways a more effective source of light). According to this line of
reasoning, changes to the structural system were only a by-product
of the need to change the window design. Inherent structural
problems within the original design had never been considered,
despite the fact that anyone visiting the cathedral today will see
that the benefit of the larger clerestory windows has been over-
rated; Notre-Dame remains a dark building. Our model study,
however, yielded indications of a *structural* rationale for the alter-
ation of the first buttressing system.

Initially undertaken to confirm the technological validity of
the new reconstruction, photoelastic modeling revealed some un-
anticipated critically stressed regions in the wall fabric (figure
4.10). With loadings simulating the distributed dead weight and
the effects of high winds on the cathedral's walls and roof, the

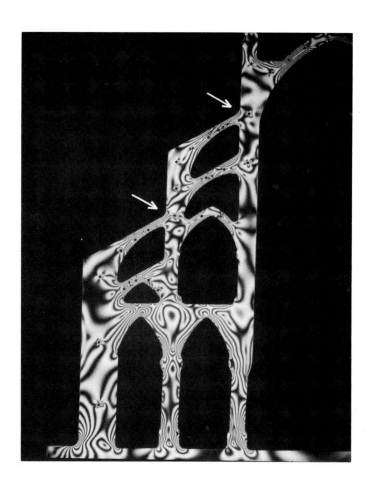

4.10
Photoelastic interference pattern in model of reconstructed Notre-Dame de Paris nave structure under simulated wind loading. Arrows denote regions of local tension.

4.11
Notre-Dame de Paris: cross-section of the nave after the thirteenth-century rebuilding.

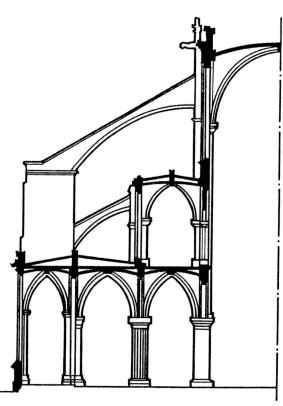

model results indicated that the nave structure would have been subjected to only moderate levels of compressive stress. But two local regions of tension were also indicated on the windward buttressing, both occurring at points where the upper ends of the flyer arches abutted the clerestory and gallery walls. During heavy storms, such as modern records indicate could have taken place from time to time during the forty-odd-year life of the original configuration, some cracking in the weak lime-mortar grouted joints would have become apparent. Because these tensions were highly localized, however, it is doubtful that major problems with the fabric would have arisen. On the other hand, repairs—including the repointing of all the affected joints—would have had to be made promptly after every great storm to prevent more general deterioration. The affected regions were not easily accessible, and the need for constant observation and regular maintenance suggests that it was more than coincidence that these very regions were eliminated in the thirteenth-century rebuilding of the nave buttressing (figure 4.11).

Further confirmation of real or recognized potential structural problems in the nave of Notre-Dame is provided by the buttress details of other buildings constructed contemporaneously or only a few years later. The evidence of the two giant cathedrals at Bourges and Chartres, whose construction was begun in 1194 and 1195 respectively, suggests that the problems we have identified at Paris were recognized by other builders early on. Hence, Notre-Dame may well have been the initial model for determining the subsequent modifications of the buttressing system of Bourges and Chartres. And, in turn, modifications comparable to those introduced at Bourges and Chartres provided the experimental data for the builders who later altered the nave buttressing of Notre-Dame de Paris itself in the 1220s.[10]

Bourges and Chartres

Because it has five aisles throughout and has a similar ground plan, Bourges Cathedral has often been linked to Notre-Dame de Paris. Yet the elevation of Bourges was unique: instead of expressing its great height of 36 meters (118 feet) from floor to keystone by enlarging the high clerestory, the builders dramatically elevated the inner side aisles and main piers to display a complete, three-story elevation through the main arcade. Robert Branner, author of the only modern monograph on Bourges Cathedral, took some pains to disassociate its design from that of Notre-Dame de

Paris.[11] Details of the Bourges design such as the clerestory windows and the double-walled passages (also found, for example, in the early Gothic cathedral at Laon) convinced Branner that the masters of Bourges were trained not in Paris but rather to the northeast of the Ile-de-France, in the Aisne River Valley. Other characteristic features of Bourges, including the five continuous aisles and the alternating widths of the piers, Branner noted, need not have derived directly from Paris, as there were many earlier buildings elsewhere that could have been sources. Nonetheless, a comparison of our Notre-Dame nave reconstruction with a section taken through the Bourges choir (figure 4.2) reveals striking similarities in *spatial* proportioning between the two designs. Indeed, this coincidence provides additional corroboration of the Paris reconstruction, and it also disaffirms Branner's contention. Furthermore, the Bourges designer seems to have used the Paris nave lighting scheme, but with far greater efficacy. Light from the lower clerestory, which is more effective than light from a higher region of the wall (as explained in note 7), is transmitted directly to the Bourges interior without interference from gallery floors, and the quality of the resulting light is extraordinary.

The Bourges choir, completed in 1214, is a simple, light, and daring structure that is sound both in principle and, as its survival attests, in its fabric. Modeling has indicated that, in spite of the extreme lightness of its construction, maximum stresses within its structure are only one-half to two-thirds the magnitude of those found in other large Gothic churches.[12] And in critical regions of the structure where tensile stresses usually tend to develop, such as at the ends of the flying buttresses, the structure performs at least as well as any other large Gothic church that we have studied in detail.

The soundness of the Bourges structure derives in part from the fact that its cross-section is more triangular in form than those of the classic High Gothic buildings, such as Chartres and Reims (see figure 4.2). A triangular section with a wide, stable base is less likely to suffer from the kind of lateral deformation that produces bending and accompanying tensile stresses. Since the function of the flying buttresses is to counteract horizontal thrusts from vaulting and from wind loadings and to transmit these to the ground, the steeper the angle at which the flying buttress can counter the thrust, the shorter the distance the forces must travel. Also, when the slope of the flyer is made steeper, the flyer itself is

4.12
*Bourges Cathedral: southeast flank and
ultralight flyers.*

subject to lower bending forces. Furthermore, a significant economy results because the upright buttresses can now be made shorter to meet the lower ends of the flying buttresses. This is evident from a comparison of the weights of the buttressing of the two similarly dimensioned cathedrals of Chartres and Bourges: about 1,000 tons for a Chartres buttress versus 400 tons for a buttress used at Bourges.

The technical studies have helped to give Bourges a new place within the development of Gothic architecture. Yet questions about its unique design remain unanswered. How, at this early stage in the development of Gothic buttressing, did the master of Bourges arrived at such an efficient design? And why, in spite of its evident technical success, were the lightness and the steepness of the Bourges choir buttressing not emulated in other High Gothic churches? Even the buttressing system of the Bourges nave, erected in a pattern similar to that of the choir during a later campaign of construction, used more massive flyers. Indeed, it was not until long after its appearance at Bourges, in a few late Gothic churches, that the Bourges type of buttressing was used again. Fortunately, the key providing the answers to these questions can be found in Branner's monograph.

In his archaeological analysis of the Bourges wall fabric, Branner observed that the design and handling of the architectural details in the high clerestory are different from the treatment of comparable details in the inner aisle clerestory. These changes are only the most visible signs of a series of design and construction differences, which include details in the zones of the two clerestory wall passages.[13] Because the later stages did not follow the lines of the early construction, Branner inferred that the original project called for just a single flight of flyers to support the nave clerestory. If the upper flyers from the outer flight are removed as well, and the supporting buttress shortened accordingly (figure 4.13), the original buttressing reveals a pattern very close to that of the Paris nave, strongly suggesting that the original inspiration for the Bourges buttressing came directly from Paris.

Although we do not know the exact date of the change in design at Bourges, it can be assumed from the relatively fast pace of the choir construction that the decision was taken shortly before, or at the commencement of, the raising of the full superstructure in the years 1208–1214. By this time, most of the completed nave of Notre-Dame de Paris, with its two-tiered flying buttresses, had already been standing for at least a decade; and, as

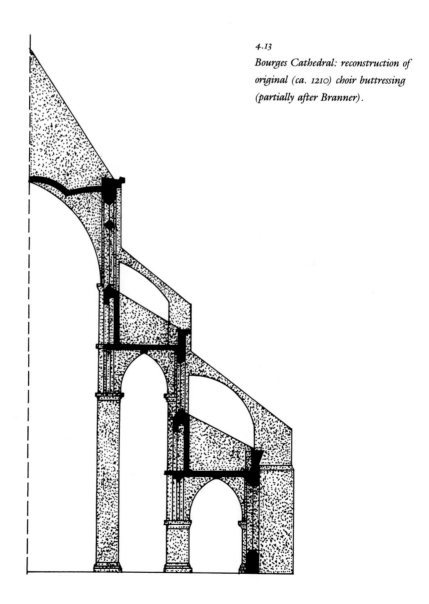

4.13
Bourges Cathedral: reconstruction of
original (ca. 1210) choir buttressing
(partially after Branner).

we have already observed, it is very likely that the clerestory walls exhibited problems caused by inadequate wind bracing. The decision to construct new flying buttresses having higher abutment against the clerestory wall was probably being discussed by the second decade of the thirteenth century, and there is every reason to believe that this information would have been transmitted to the building site at Bourges. The addition of the aisle upper flyer, the bifurcation of the main flying buttresses, and the raising of the elevation of the abutment of the upper flyer with the high clerestory wall can all be viewed as precautionary measures taken in anticipation of similar problems. As it turned out, moving the buttress abutment upward was especially prudent. Modeling has indicated that the abutment region is the most critical one of the entire Bourges structure and that a lower intersection between the flyer and the clerestory wall would have exacerbated the potential for problems within the masonry.

These efficient, highly sloped flying buttresses, then, were brought into being as part of a pragmatic redesign of the cathedral's structure in response to the Bourges master's generally increased awareness of the wind's effect on tall buildings. Such knowledge, before the full raising of Bourges, would have come only from Paris. As to the possible reasons that the flying buttresses of Bourges were not emulated in other contemporary buildings, one is that these buttresses were viewed in their time as a "technical fix" and therefore as not fully appropriate for monumental architecture. Another reason may well be their identification with an "older" style of building (see the discussion of vaulting later in this section). Whatever the cause, the main line of High Gothic development seems to have bypassed Bourges in favor of the contemporary cathedral of Chartres.

Begun almost simultaneously with Bourges, and at a similar scale (its high vaults are 34.5 meters [113 feet] above the floor), Chartres Cathedral was virtually complete by as early as 1221. The return from a four-story to a three-story elevation with a narrow, middle triforium passage and greatly enlarged clerestory windows which drop well below the level of the springing of the vaults (figure 4.14) are the major innovations of the Chartres design. It has been generally assumed that the basis of this achievement was the Chartres builders' realization of the full potential of the new system of flying buttresses. I have observed, however, that the buttressing of the Chartres nave, which uses the equivalent of three separate flying buttresses (figure 4.15) and a heavy spur (the

4.14
Chartres Cathedral: northeast transept wall and quadripartite vaulting.

4.15

Chartres Cathedral nave: flying buttress.

4.16

*Chartres Cathedral nave: system of
flying buttress without upper flyers (after
Viollet-le-Duc).*

triangular wall under the side aisle roof illustrated in figure 4.2) to support the wall, is relatively ponderous—even somewhat clumsy—from a technological vantage point.

Long before that observation was made, questions were raised about the dating and the function of the uppermost flyers. They spring awkwardly from the top of the buttress, and they cut through a projecting foliated cornice at the junction with the nave wall (figures 4.15 and 4.16). No one has doubted their not being intended as part of the original design scheme, but it was not clear whether the flyers were added as an afterthought during the campaign of primary construction or after the famous *Expertise* of 1316 (a report, by a group of technical consultants who traveled to Chartres from Paris, that included imprecise recommendations to "attend to the buttresses"). Modern reinterpretation of the *Expertise* indicates that only pointing of the buttresses was wanted.[14] And modeling of the nave structure, both with and without the upper flyers in place, reveals that the relatively light upper flyer is not fully effective in reducing local tension caused by high winds in the clerestory wall just above the junction of the top main flyer. It was therefore an unlikely corrective for an obvious design fault seen by the Paris experts, which argues that the upper flyers were erected near the end of the original building campaign.[15]

In view of the evidence of Paris and Bourges, the upper flyers at Chartres would seem to have been erected as a precautionary device to ward off the problems encountered in earlier buildings as a result of high winds. The fact that modeling has shown that the upper flyers are not fully effective also points to their having been placed for this purpose rather than to solve a pressing structural problem. Furthermore, despite having provided a relatively massive supporting structure, the master of Chartres may well have felt concern for the greatly enlarged clerestory walls. And the subsequent trend toward taller clerestories and higher vault springing along with less solid clerestory walls, in seeming defiance of the thrust of the lofty vaults, was to become a definitive stylistic and structural feature of the French High Gothic cathedral.

Before Chartres, vaults sprang from a solid wall at a point below the base of the clerestory. With few exceptions, square-plan vaults of sexpartite figuration (figure 4.17) were used in the main bays of the larger Gothic churches, including the cathedrals of Paris and Bourges. After Chartres, and evidently following its

4.17

Bourges Cathedral: sexpartite vaulting.

example, there was a complete shift to rectangular-plan, quadripartite vaults, sprung from a point well above the clerestory base to cover soaring interior spaces (compare figures 4.14 and 4.17). A causal relationship between the development of the raised High Gothic clerestory supported by flying buttresses and the shift in vault configuration seems obvious, yet the literature on Gothic architecture has been rather vague on this point.

Not surprisingly, stylistic explanations predominate in art-historical scholarship, where it is implicitly understood that the use of sexpartite vaults arose from the introduction of alternating nave piers.[16] Since with sexpartite vaulting the number of vault ribs springing from the piers is alternately one and three, this system is claimed to be a logical visual complement to alternating piers. By the same reasoning, the stylistic theories attribute the adoption of quadripartite vaulting to the introduction of uniform, non-alternating piers. If it is accepted that alternating piers are visually compatible with sexpartite vaults, and uniform piers with quadripartite vaults, it is problematic, nevertheless, to use this observation to explain the sudden adoption of quadripartite vaults in High Gothic cathedrals. It would be difficult to show that such stylistic unity actually was a major concern for the medieval builders, particularly since both Paris and Chartres are exceptions to this schema.

Nor have constructional theories provided adequate explanation. These are generally based on the premise that quadripartite vaults were easier to build than sexpartite vaults. Some scholars, however, have concluded that the centering was more difficult to erect for quadripartite vaulting than for sexpartite. It has also been suggested that the High Gothic builders adopted quadripartite vaults because they were lighter than sexpartite vaults.[17] But a series of model studies of ribbed vaulting performed at Princeton to determine the structural role of the vault rib also revealed that the weight of a sexpartite vault was actually significantly *less* than the weight of quadripartite vaults covering the same area.[18] The finding that the thirteenth-century builders, who generally favored light construction, chose to construct heavier vaults over increasingly slender piers and walls in the tallest churches did nothing to clarify the enigma of the vault transition.

The question was resolved, though, by examining the forces necessary to support the vaults during construction. Consider first the salient structural feature of Gothic vaulting: the "focusing" of the distributed forces within the vaults at the points of vault support along the clerestory wall. There are three components of this focused force resultant at the springing: (1) a downward, vertical component equal to the weight of the ribbed vaulting supported by the clerestory wall, which in turn is carried by the piers of the main arcade; (2) a lateral, outward, horizontal component tending to overturn the clerestory wall, but resisted in a mature Gothic church by flying buttresses; and (3) a longitudinal, horizontal component against the adjacent bay along the axis of the church. This last force is ordinarily stabilized by the adjacent bay of vaulting, whose longitudinal component acts in the opposite direction to that of its neighbor, or by such devices as a pair of massive towers at the end of the nave. In effect, the completed bays of vaulting all "lean" against one another.

From this brief description of the mechanics of vault support, it is evident that mature Gothic buttressing can readily support any reasonable form of vaulting, sexpartite or quadripartite. (A quadripartite model is illustrated in figure 2.5.) A different condition is present, however, during the *construction* of the vaults, which was generally carried out, one bay at a time, on movable centering. Since the erection of the vaulting was necessarily preceded by the erection of the piers, the walls, and the flying buttresses, the vertical weight and the outward horizontal thrusts of the vault bay after its centering was removed were resisted by the same structural elements as in the finished church. On the other hand, the longitudinal thrust along the axis of the church (figure 4.18) at this stage of construction must have been supported by

4.18
Comparative plans of quadripartite and sexpartite vaulting, showing longitudinal and lateral components of vault reactions.

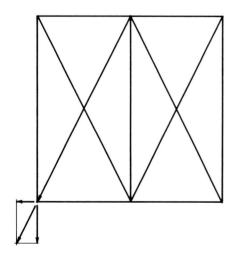

QUADRIPARTITE

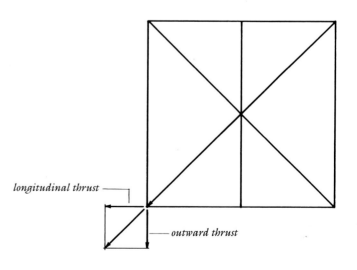

longitudinal thrust

outward thrust

SEXPARTITE

the celerestory wall, and likely by timber props, since an adjacent vaulting bay to provide stabilization was not yet in place. As the springing of the vaults was carried upward from the base of the clerestory in later buildings, coping with this thrust at higher elevations became a far more serious problem of construction. The sexpartite-vaulting model corresponding to Bourges indicated a longitudinal thrust of 19,000 kg (42,000 lb). For the equivalent quadripartite vaulting of Chartres (from modeling based on vaulting from the choir of Cologne Cathedral), the longitudinal thrust is indicated to be only 9,000 kg (20,000 lb)—a force reduction of more than 50 percent in comparison with sexpartite vaulting.

The constructional problems presented by the intensity of these longitudinal thrusts do not appear to have been crucial in the early Gothic churches, as the vault springing could be anchored in the typically massive walls below the clerestory. The countering of this force became an acute problem only with the demand for greater clerestory height and the accompanying fenestration, as at Chartres, which brought an end to the practice of having the vault spring from a solid wall. Thin clerestory walls could have displayed cracking, even if braced with temporary timber falsework, and this might well have brought the conviction to the Gothic builders that the walls were unable to resist forces of such magnitude. As with flying buttresses, quadripartite vaulting was probably adopted in High Gothic churches for structural reasons; the flying buttresses provided support for the outward thrusts of the high vaults, while the quadripartite vaulting reduced longitudinal thrusts to manageable levels during construction.

The observation that it was impractical to have sexpartite vaulting spring from a point above the base of the clerestory also sheds new light on the long-discussed comparison of the designs of Chartres and Bourges. The main reason for the ascendancy of Chartres, according to Robert Branner, is that its design could be reordered to suit almost any site, whereas the Bourges scheme could be adopted only as whole.[19] Now a corollary can be appended: The supremacy of the Chartres model was also ensured by the fact that the sexpartite vaulting of Bourges would not allow the clerestory in a building of that scale to be enlarged. On the other hand, the flexibility of the Chartres design—particularly that of its quadripartite vaulting—could well satisfy the Gothic desire for great clerestory height.

The adoption of quadripartite vaulting allowed stone structures to become more truly skeletal. And even if the upper flyers of Chartres were not fully effective, they appear to have pointed the way toward efficacious flying-buttress placement in the classic High Gothic churches that followed. In these buildings—as exemplified in that next vast essay in Gothic architecture, the Cathedral of Reims, begun in 1210—a lower tier of flyers was positioned to resist the outward thrust of the stone vaulting over the nave, and an upper tier of flyers braced the high clerestory wall and the tall timber roof above the vaults against wind loadings.

Reims

The classic phase of the High Gothic is generally agreed to have been established in the design of Reims by its first master, Jean d'Orbais. Although local political instability seems to have slowed the pace of construction in the 1230s, the choir and the transept began to be used for church services in 1241.[20] And by the 1250s five bays (of a final total of eight) of the nave were standing. Three succeeding architects took charge of the project before it was completed in 1289, but their work held generally faithful to Jean d'Orbais's design, so that the entire building is remarkably unified in aspect.

A key element in the exterior visual massing of Reims is the array of great pinnacles topping the buttresses (figure 4.19). Pinnacles had been used earlier on buttresses, but never so emphatically. According to Jean Bony, "these tall spirelets, each sheltering the winged figure of an angel, are not merely a lovely three-dimensional motif which gives firmness and unity to the upper part of the buttresses, nor is their end simply to accentuate the cadence of the bays: still more important is the horizontal continuity they create all around the building by their succession. . . . through their precision of form and their crystalline density, [they] express within themselves the laws that organize the whole structure."[21]

It is doubtful that the influential early-twentieth-century architectural critic Pol Abraham would have taken exception to Bony's elegant description, but Abraham did cite Reims in a list of buildings whose pinnacle placement he considered structurally detrimental. According to Abraham, the pinnacle, in addition to its beauty, can be a useful structural device only if it augments the stability of a buttress, as determined by a vertical line taken through its center and also passing through the center of gravity of the buttress.[22] Accordingly, he argues, the placing of a pinnacle close to the exterior edge of a buttress diminishes stability. But the long-time presence of the affected buildings attests to the fact that they are not lacking in stability. Abraham did not take into

4.19
Reims Cathedral: buttressing of the nave.

account that the weight of a pinnacle provides additional compressive force to the stones below it, helping to consolidate them and thereby helping to prevent their lateral sliding, or shearing, under the action of the horizontal component of thrust from the flying buttress (as illustrated in figure 2.1c). This function, moreover, does not depend upon the exact position of the pinnacle on the pier buttress; it depends only on the additional weight provided by the pinnacle. In some instances, too, I have discovered that the pinnacle acts to "prestress" the buttress by adding compression over a local region that would otherwise be in tension from the effect of high winds. (See the discussion of the Amiens pinnacle later in this chapter.)

A pinnacle is relatively light in comparison with the great weight of a buttress, so its effect on the overall stability of the buttress is small and often appears to have been ignored in design. On the other hand, at Reims (whose 38 m [124 ft] high vaults are only 2 meters taller than those of Bourges) the designer seems to have had some anxiety about stability; he took pains to mitigate the effect of the pinnacle loading. A typical Reims buttress pinnacle

(figure 4.20)—consisting of a central octagonal spire, slotted and hollowed out so that its net volume is about 70 percent of its gross, and four small solid spires of triangular section—is estimated to weigh 29 tons. The weight of the winged angel statue, its base, its entablature, and the surrounding columns was estimated to be 23 tons, giving a total weight of 52 tons for the assembly. This weight is almost exactly equal to the weight of the volume of stone removed from the buttress (estimated at 54 tons) to create the aedicula that shelters the statue. Thus, the net effect of the Reims pinnacle on the overall buttress stability is effectively nil.

This balancing of mass seems rather sophisticated for medieval design; however, the observation is supported by the presence of solid decorative pinnacles in other parts of the cathedral, such those placed along the west facade (figure 4.21). Evidently, the structure of Reims was designed with the same premeditation expressed in the precise visual organization of the entire building. This deliberateness may have been a response to the further reduction of the walls (the clerestory windows of Reims are appreciably larger in area than those of Chartres), but perhaps it was also a reaction to the earlier problems at Paris.

A quantitative evaluation of the structural action of the Reims pinnacles was performed by testing a small-scale photoelastic model of the nave structure. Scaled loadings were applied to the model (as in figure 4.4) in a pattern similar to full-scale, dead-weight loadings in two tests—the first without the simulated weight of the pinnacle and statue assemblies, the second with the full dead weight of all loadings—to produce the interference pattern shown in figure 4.22. In a third test, the model was loaded with simulated wind loads based on long-term wind data from local meteorological records.

Combining the model results from the first and third tests (representing dead weight and wind, but with pinnacles and statues unloaded) and from the second and third tests (full dead weight and wind), and scaling these to the full-scale structure, revealed that compression prevails in both cases. A few local regions of tension were observed near the ends of the flying buttresses (caused by bending of the flyers—not unusual, as the frequent repointing of almost all flyers demonstrates) and along the external edges of the buttresses, within and just below the aedicula. The stresses in the flying buttress were not affected by the addition of the weights of the pinnacles and the statues, but amelioration of

4.20
*Reims Cathedral: "balanced" pinnacles
on nave buttresses.*

4.21
*Reims Cathedral: "decorative" pinnacles
on west facade.*

Photoelastic interference pattern in model of Reims Cathedral nave structure under stimulated dead-weight loading.

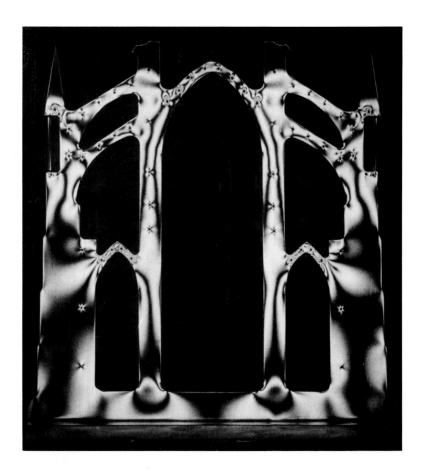

tensile stresses in the other regions was indicated when the weights of the pinnacles and the statues were activated. Within the aedicula of the windward buttress, under the action of high winds, the small tensile stress present without the weight of pinnacle and statue was reduced almost to zero. Just below the aedicula of the leeward buttress, the tension, which is caused mainly by dead weight and is actually little affected by wind action, completely changed over to compression. The low magnitude of the indicated tensile stresses indicates that these are not very critical, even without the weight of the pinnacles and the statues. Nevertheless, the builders could still have become aware of their existence by observing small fissures in the newly set mortar. The additional weights of the pinnacles and statues, according to the test results, would certainly have removed any trace of such cracking.

If the buttress pinnacles of Reims do play a dual role of art and structure, then the local tensile stresses in the buttresses eliminated by the action of the pinnacles are not large enough to have been worrisome. This observation, as well as the elaborate sculptural treatment of the buttress, points to the conclusion that the pinnacle arrangement of Reims was predetermined rather than being a solution to a pressing structural problem. However, the evidence from the analysis of the next giant building in this series, Amiens Cathedral, leads to the opposite conclusion.

Amiens

The Cathedral of Amiens, begun in 1220, is generally considered the *summa* of the French High Gothic. Robert de Luzarches set the course of the overall design, and under his direction the 42 m (138 ft) tall nave was completed by about 1233. In contrast to the usual practice of first constructing an eastern choir (the principal setting of liturgical ceremony) and then constructing the nave devoted to the lay worshipper, Amiens was built from west to east. The high vaults of the choir were not in place until 1269, and by then the earlier High Gothic pattern had been superseded by the newer Rayonnant style (the term derives from the characteristic tracery of the windows). In this phase of building, designers may have felt that the major structural problems of the Gothic had been solved, and they seem to have been concerned primarily with the handling of vast areas of glass held in place by slender stone tracery. Yet while some areas of technical development slowed, there was an increased refinement in stonecutting and a new precision in architectural draftsmanship.

Understanding the stability that flying buttresses gave to the walls, designers had earlier removed the transverse spur buttressing from behind the triforium zone midway up the wall. With the spur removed, the triforium area was freed of external structure, and soon afterward it was opened to the exterior to admit light (figure 4.24). This opening up to daylight, which also had the effect of raising the springing of the high vaults to an extreme height above a solid wall, became a characteristic feature of Rayonnant design.

Amiens is the largest of the French cathedrals that have survived without extensive rebuilding or any taint of the kind of structural failure associated with Beauvais, the only French cathedral that exceeded its vaulting height. Although its nave buttressing follows the pattern of Reims (figure 4.2), Amiens is in every way a much lighter, more daring building. The different treatment of the pinnacles, which are placed on the extreme outer edges of solid buttresses, provides a further indication of the diverse approaches to structure taken by the respective designers. And of course Amiens appears on Pol Abraham's "endangered" list.

The nave section of the church as originally constructed provided the basis of a photoelastic model that was tested under high-wind and simulated dead-weight loadings. The modeling did not include the effect of the weight of the pinnacles, which was analytically taken into account at a later stage. When the results of both tests were compared, only a few local regions of tension were noted: at the ends of the flying buttresses (as is usual), and along the outer edge of the leeward, upright buttresses, just under the pinnacles. In the absence of the pinnacle, the buttress is subjected to a level of tension under the loading of both wind and dead weight that would have produced cracking in the weak lime mortar; the addition of the pinnacle on the outer edge of the buttress brings it fully into a state of compression. It seems, therefore, that the pinnacles of Amiens, unlike the pinnacles of Reims, were placed with exactly this structural function in mind.[23]

We stand in awe at the ingenuity of the Gothic builders in a pre-scientific age. How can the sophistication of the placement of the Amiens pinnacle so that it prestresses the outside edge of the upright buttress be explained? The only reasonable answer is that the medieval builder had available an experimental modeling method parallel to our modern one but used the full-scale building as his model. Since the cathedrals were built over a relatively

4.24
Amiens Cathedral: illuminated triforium passage of north transept.

4.25
Amiens Cathedral: pinnacles atop nave buttresses.

long time in periodic cycles during the warmer, brighter "construction seasons" (from about the beginning of April through the end of October), tensile cracking, caused either by high winds or by the removal of temporary supports, could have been observed in the newly set mortar between the stones of the bays completed first. As a result, design changes could have been made in later bays to eliminate the cause of the cracking. These successive modifications would then have been the source of structural innovation.

It is interesting to speculate how this full-scale experimental technique might have been used to rectify other pitfalls in Gothic design. For example, the tensile cracking of the mortar almost always present at the ends of flying buttresses must have been just as evident to the medieval builders as it is to restorers today. The solution for reducing bending at the ends of the flying buttresses, however, is not as obvious as that for preventing tensile cracking at the top of an upright buttress (i.e., the placing of additional stone). From studying the structure of Bourges we know that the bending can be reduced by increasing the slope of the flying buttresses, but the medieval designers either did not recognize the efficiency of the Bourges solution or did not wish to alter the appearance of the classic High Gothic structure. The following study of the cathedral of Beauvais demonstrates the import of that decision; but even so, the collapse of a major building might well have been avoided if cracking in the mortar caused by tension had been observed in time.

Beauvais

Much of the interest in Beauvais Cathedral has been focused on the height of its vaults—48 meters (158 feet)—and on its collapse in 1284. The work of the unknown first master, begun in 1225, was concluded before 1245, by which time the choir below the main triforium was complete. A second master may have worked for a short period, and around 1250 or 1255 a third master took over the work and carried it on until 1272, erecting the buttressing and the high choir vaults to a greater elevation than intended by the first master.[24]

In 1284, all or part of the high vaults over the original three straight bays of the choir collapsed. The repairs, completed by about 1337, included replacement of all the original quadripartite vaults by unconventional rectangular-plan sexpartite vaults (figure 4.27) and the erection of additional unbuttressed piers in the three bays (figure 4.28). Work ceased during the Hundred Years War,

Beauvais Cathedral: apse buttressing.

4.27
Beauvais Cathedral: fourteenth-century choir vaulting.

4.28
Beauvais Cathedral: north wall of choir and apse.

and the transept was not begun until about 1500. Between 1564 and 1569, before work on the nave was far advanced, a gigantic stone tower, some 150 meters (490 feet) in height, was erected over the crossing. This tower collapsed in 1573, and although the damage from this disaster was repaired by 1578 the tower itself was not replaced. No major construction was undertaken after that date; the cathedral was left truncated.

Many theories have been advanced to explain why the vaults fell in 1284, but none of them have stood the test of close archaeological and technological scrutiny. One commonly held view is that the high vaults, like the Tower of Babel, touched the limits of construction in stone.[25] But there is no intrinsic structural principle that would hold Gothic bay construction to a height of 50 meters, as is attested by the well-being of the repaired structure of Beauvais. In the absence of any evidence to suggest that the failure of the vaults in 1284 was caused by settlement of the foundations or by any unusual loading such as that from an earthquake, we undertook wind and dead-load photoelastic modeling in an attempt to understand better the structure of the cathedral and possibly to arrive at a conclusive explanation for the collapse.

The experiments confirmed our reservations about previous theories of the vaults' collapse.[26] They indicated, for example, that structural problems were not likely in the main supporting piers. But the dead-load experiment revealed that the intermediate buttresses (the slender uprights supporting the centers of the flying buttresses in the choir section, illustrated in figure 4.2) were bent by horizontal forces large enough to initiate cracking just above the side aisles and just below the junction with the lower flyers. When tensile stress on the exterior portion of the leeward intermediate buttress caused by wind loading was added to the tension already present from the dead loading, the indicated total tensile stress on the inside edge above the aisle was about 10 times the tensile strength of lime mortar; and it was only slightly less on the outside edge below the flyers. Moreover, since the tensile stress on the buttresses would have alternated as the wind changed direction, cracks could have developed on both sides—and because of the locations of these cracks, they would have been difficult to detect. The upper critical regions, near the flyers, would not have been readily accessible, and the lower cracks were concealed by a gabled side aisle roof.

Though the experimental results were derived from an estimated "worst wind," winds of lower velocity could still have produced the predicted cracking. Since wind forces vary as the square of wind speed, two-thirds of the speed of the worst wind would produce roughly half the load simulated in the test. The tensile stresses produced by such winds still exceed the capacity of unreinforced masonry construction. Less violent storms that might have occurred relatively often, therefore, could have cracked the slender upright buttresses. Perhaps even within the twelve-year period following the completion of the choir, cracking under alternating wind loads caused an intermediate buttress to deteriorate so badly that the horizontal forces acting on it slid a section from its support. If an intermediate buttress had collapsed, the system of flying buttresses above it would have been unsupported at its center, causing the flyers to fall and allowing the horizontal thrust of the high vaults to push out a section of the clerestory wall and trigger the sequential fall of the vaults.

In the aftermath of the collapse, it is likely that the master in charge of rebuilding Beauvais understood that the intermediate buttress absorbed some of the transmitted thrust from the flying buttresses. The replacement of its quadripartite vaults with sexpartite vaults can be interpreted as an attempt to reduce the horizontal forces, because the extra piers needed to support the new vault would have absorbed some of the wind loads on the clerestory and hence reduced the loads transmitted to the intermediate buttresses through the flyers. Moreover, the four western intermediate buttresses (two on the north and two on the south of the choir), which were rebuilt after the collapse, are far larger in section than those in the hemicycle. There is also a third set of flyers (see section in figure 4.2) abutting some of the intermediate buttresses, and on those buttresses that lack the support of additional flyers there are iron bars or traces of them in similar positions. The extra sets of flyers and bars seem to have been intended mainly to support the intermediate buttresses, especially those around the hemicycle (figure 4.29). The mode of reconstruction of the choir would thus seem to bear out this hypothesis.

If we assume that this analysis of the cause of the collapse is correct, can we now point to a design blunder on the part of any of the Beauvais masters? In retrospect, the raising of the high vaults by the third master turns out to have been a mistake; but perhaps the fundamental error in the design was the acceptance of

4.29
Beauvais Cathedral: buttressing of upper hemicycle.

the classic Gothic buttressing system, with its very tall buttresses and its relatively horizontal flyers. A system of buttressing more in keeping with the profile of Bourges would have reduced the great height of the intermediate buttresses and stiffened the entire structure. The masters of Beauvais were not alone in making this choice (which may have been motivated largely by formal considerations); however, the scale of Beauvais left fewer technical options, and their failure to profit fully from the experience with the buttressing of Bourges exacted a heavy cost.

The year 1284 is often taken as the turning point in the development of Gothic building. After the events at Beauvais, it is generally assumed, the designers of large churches were more timid and less willing to carry out experiments in structure such as those that had produced the classic High Gothic cathedral. But this interpretation does not take into account the concurrent beginning of a long cycle of economic depression and social and religious upheaval in Western Europe.[27] The erosion of the financial underpinning of these great buildings was probably a far greater determinant of the future course of Gothic architecture than any erosion of the designers' nerve. And in any event, structural experimentation in tall buildings did continue in other regions well into the fourteenth century (for example, the high vaults of the great cathedral at Palma, Majorca, begun ca. 1357, are 2 meters taller than those of Amiens).[28] Yet the vitality of design and construction in the fourteenth century cannot be compared to that of the thirteenth; nor has any period before the industrial revolution matched the building activity that took place, particularly in northern France, between the middle of the twelfth century and the middle of the thirteenth.

5

Christopher Wren,
Seventeenth-Century Science, and
Great Renaissance Domes

The Renaissance of the fifteenth and sixteenth centuries witnessed the displacement of the master builders as the principal designers of major buildings by artist-architects, typified by the goldsmith Filippo Brunelleschi (1377–1446) and the sculptor Michelangelo (1475–1564).[1] Like the master builders, the artist-architects eschewed theoretical mechanics, sometimes in favor of a revived hope that visual aesthetics might be founded on a system parallel to the arithmetical principles of musical harmony discovered by the ancients.[2]

In the seventeenth century the vocation of architecture was revised once again; now it was scientist-architects who received commissions. Guarino Guarini (1624–1683), an Italian mathematician, worked mainly in Turin, where his major works included the Church of S. Lorenzo (1666–1679), the Chapel of the Sudario (1667–1692), and the Palazzo Carignano (1679–1692).[3] In France, Claude Perrault (1613–1688) was a physician and animal anatomist until late in life, when he was drawn into the design of the Louvre and the observatory of the Paris Academy.[4] And in England, Christopher Wren (1632–1723) and Robert Hooke (1635–1703), after helping to establish the Royal Society, collaborated as chief architect and city surveyor in rebuilding the churches and public buildings of London after the Great Fire of 1666.[5]

Much of the material in this chapter was derived from Harold Dorn and R. Mark, "The Architecture of Christopher Wren," *Scientific American* 245 (July 1981): 160–173. For historical background on Wren, see Stephen Wren, ed., *Parentalia, or Memoirs of the Family of Wren* (London: T. Osborn, 1750). On Wren's wider architectural oeuvre, see Eduard F. Sekler, *Wren and His Place in European Architecture* (Macmillan, 1956).

Hanc Tabulam invenit & incepit Anton: Verrio Perfecerunt Gothofredus Kneller & Jac: Thornhill Equites.

Seventeenth-century European civilization was also swept by
the crest of the Scientific Revolution, which transformed science
as an enterprise and revised the cognitive systems of the separate
sciences. Some of the achievements of that revolution promised to
assist the architect in the art of building, and one may properly
enquire whether the promise was kept.

In Galileo's *Dialogues Concerning Two New Sciences*, published
in 1638, the more heralded of the two sciences—dynamics—was
the subject of the second dialogue; the first (at least, in the order
in which the dialogues appear in the masterpiece composed during Galileo's final years under house arrest) was on the strength of
materials.[6] Although he presented that new science as natural philosophy rather than as engineering mechanics, it is known from
his correspondence that when Galileo had first discovered its principles, 30 years previously, he had recognized that they constituted
a "science very necessary in making machines and all kinds of
buildings."[7]

In architectural theory as well as in scientific research, the
seventeenth century seemed ripe for a merger of science and the
art of building. Henry Wotton, a poet, critic, and playwright who
served as the English ambassador to Venice and was keenly alert
to the scientific currents of his time, composed a volume on architecture in 1624 wherein he presented a rudimentary structural
analysis of an arch similar to one he had learned in Italy.[8] Despite
these preliminary steps toward affiliation, it was only in the
nineteenth century that the merger finally took hold, abetted by
the introduction of new construction materials to which the old
rules of building no longer applied and by the establishment of
architecture and engineering as university subjects. In the age of
Wren, the intellectual innovations of the Scientific Revolution
were still unable to revise the procedures of architectural design.
And Wren's career reflected the historical process to a remarkable
degree.

At an early age Wren was strongly influenced by ecclesiastical traditions, a circumstance that would be later reflected in his
architecture. His father became Dean of the Collegiate Chapel of
Windsor, and an uncle Bishop of Ely. At the University of Oxford, which Wren entered in 1649, he came under the influence
of John Wilkins, who was later to become Bishop of Chester. At
Oxford, too, Wren began to display the mathematical ability for
which Isaac Newton later praised him (along with Isaac Wallis
and Christian Huygens) as one of "the greatest Geometers of our

times."[9] In 1657, at the age of 25, Wren received the professorship of astronomy at Gresham College in London; four years later, he was elected Savilian Professor of Astronomy at Oxford, a chair he held until 1673. In 1662 the Royal Society was formally established, and Wren, a charter member and one of its leading lights, became its president 18 years later. Indeed, Wren had drafted a preamble to the Society's charter of incorporation, and its utilitarian bias indicates that Wren's attitude toward science was already directed toward the promotion of the practical arts. Among the functions of the society, he wrote, would be "the Advancement of Natural Experimental Philosophy, especially those parts of it which concern the Encrease of Commerce, by the Addition of useful Inventions tending to the Ease, Profit, or Health of our Subjects."[10]

As a child Wren had displayed an interest in instruments and mechanical contrivances. At Oxford he prepared an exhibition of over fifty such devices, almost all of a practical nature and including, as Wren noted, "New Designs tending to Strength, Convenience and Beauty in Building." Throughout his long life Wren showed many signs of remarkable technical ingenuity; but far less clear is the extent to which he was a theoretical scientist or how he might have applied the science of mechanics to the art of building.

It has been argued that one of the historical distinctions between the scientist and the engineer is that the scientist has a compulsion to publish, whereas the engineer is indifferent to (even wary of) publication. On this scale Wren would appear to have been far more an engineer than a scientist; his enormous productivity and inventiveness in building, about which he published almost nothing, outweighed his slight list of publications (albeit not his reputation) in theoretical science. And even those few publications, aside from a celebrated paper on collision and impact,[11] are largely concerned with instruments and processes for grinding lenses or making perspective drawings. Nonetheless, Wren's biographers often presume that this work in structural design rested on principles of theoretical mechanics.[12]

Wren's experience in architecture may be considered to span the period from 1662, when he was commissioned to design the Sheldonian Theater at Oxford, to 1710, when St. Paul's Cathedral was completed. These two buildings, separated by almost a half-century and by scores of major commissions for city churches, restorations, libraries, hospitals, and royal residences, exhibit what are considered to be Wren's most impressive engineering solutions. They also display two prominent characteristics of Wren's approach to design. The first is his reliance (through published interpretations) on classical sources, which resulted in stylistic conservatism and generally in massive structure. (In extreme cases, as with some of the elements of St. Paul's, the structure is so excessively heavy that it diminishes the integrity of the building fabric.) Then, as if superimposed upon this, both buildings also incorporate original structural elements, which have drawn much attention and have played an important part in propagating the belief that Wren's architecture owed a substantial debt to his science. In the Sheldonian Theater, the novel element was the provision of great timber trusses to support the unprecedented 21-m (70 ft) span of the flat ceiling above the auditorium. In St. Paul's Cathedral, Wren's most admired building, it was the towering dome composed of three concentric shells. These two structures, bracketing Wren's career as an architect, may help us to reach an understanding of the relationship between Wren's science and his architecture.

The Sheldonian Theater

Gilbert Sheldon, who during the Interregnum had been expelled from his position as Warden of All Souls College, returned to Oxford with the restoration of Charles II in 1660. Although his second tenure was short (he was soon appointed Bishop of London, and later he was Archbishop of Canterbury), it was long enough for him to discourage the practice of using the college chapel for secular gatherings. Sheldon donated £12,000 for a new secular hall, and in selecting Wren as its architect he chose a Fellow of his own college who was also the nephew of one of the most renowned of the high-church royalists.

Wren based his design for the Sheldonian Theater on the Roman Theater of Marcellus as depicted in some of the editions of Serlio and Vitruvius (figure 5.2). But whereas the Roman arena-theater was semicircular and open, covered only by a canvas awning, the configuration of the Sheldonian Theater (figure 5.3) is more that of a horseshoe with polygonal walls, and it is entered through a formal south facade. Wren had to provide permanent closure because of the English climate, and he also had to make provision for the building's multiple uses: Until the middle of the

5.2

*Apse of the Sheldonian Theatre, Oxford
(1662–1666).*

5.3

*Theatre of Marcellus, Rome (from Como
Vitruvius, 1521).*

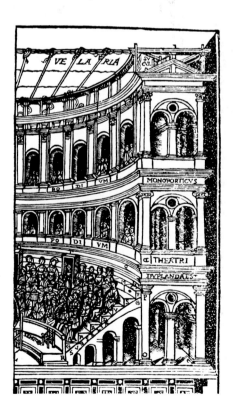

eighteenth century, the basement of the Sheldonian housed the presses of the Oxford University Press (the theater was often displayed on title pages of works from the Press), and stocks of books were stored in the attic above the auditorium.

Wren's design was notable mainly as a departure from the Gothic tradition at Oxford. Although his biographers have generally judged the Sheldonian to be less than fully mature stylistically, one feature of the building that has been universally admired from Wren's time to ours is the flat long-span auditorium ceiling, constructed without any supporting columns (figure 5.4). The ceiling painting (by Robert Streater) enhances the illusion of a Roman theater by showing a "canvas covering" pulled back from "supporting cords," revealing a "sky" with figures representing "the triumph of the Arts and the Sciences over Envy, Rapine and Ignorance."[13] The ceiling is actually supported by concealed, heavy trusses formed by joining short lengths of timber (figure 5.5). The originality of employing such trusses to create a long unobstructed ceiling can be judged from the fact that in April 1663 Wren exhibited a model of the theater before the Royal Society.[14] Nonetheless, the structure of Wren's truss is disappointing to our eyes in that it resembles more a reinforced beam (the heavy lower chord illustrated in figure 5.5) than an efficient form of truss built up from triangles to minimize bending in all its members. This disappointment is heightened because of the antiquity of the triangulated truss, and by the fact that Palladio described the application of this type of structure to a bridge as early as 1570 (figure 5.6).[15] Wren had access to Palladio's work, so either he did not appreciate the greater efficiency of the triangular truss or he did not make the connection between the structure of a bridge and that of a building. Even so, our modeling of the Sheldonian roof truss indicated that structural distress would not have been expected from stresses caused by normal loadings.[16] Perhaps, then, the weight of the stored books in the attic was abnormally large, for the original trusses needed to be replaced in 1802.

Whatever the quality of the engineering solution that Wren applied to the problem of building a flat ceiling unsupported by columns, his structure owed nothing to theoretical analysis. The theory of the truss (even of a relatively simple one) remained far in the future, and nowhere in Wren's notes or in the testimony of his contemporaries is there any indication that this design of the Sheldonian trusses was anything other than empirical. If any of

5.4

Sheldonian Theatre: interior.

5.5

Wren's roof truss for the Sheldonian Theatre.

5.6

Timber bridge truss (after Palladio, 1570).

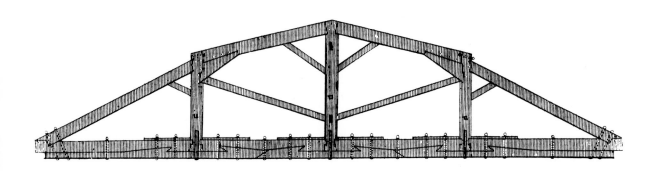

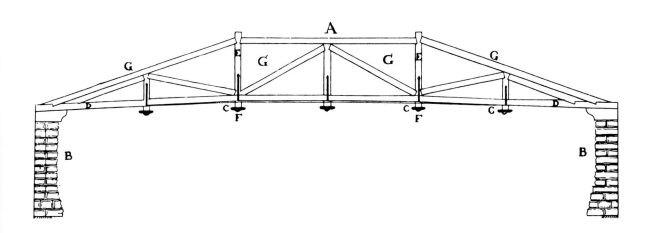

the theoretical novelties of the Scientific Revolution entered into the procedures of Wren's design studio, they cannot be detected in his work on the Sheldonian Theater—notwithstanding the conjecture by one of Wren's interpreters that the "composite bolted tie-beams [of the roof truss] suggest a background of research of which we know little."[17] The connection with science, if any, must instead be sought in the design of the structure that was to become the summit of Wren's career: St. Paul's Cathedral in London.

St. Paul's Cathedral

The Great Fire of 1666, which devastated London, also produced two salutary consequences: It halted the plague that had stuck the city in the previous year, and it provided Wren with the opportunity to deploy his genius as an architect. Within days after the fire, Wren developed a plan for reconstructing London. Although his plan was not adopted, Wren was soon appointed principal architect for the rebuilding of the city. In that capacity, and later as Surveyor General, he attended to the reconstruction of more than fifty churches. At the same time, despite the priority of restoring the local parish churches (the backbone of London's social and spiritual life), Wren directed considerable attention to the rebuilding of St. Paul's Cathedral, which had been heavily damaged in the fire.

Wren had already served an apprenticeship that had foreshadowed his role as the architect of the new cathedral. Before the Civil War, the exterior of old St. Paul's had been the object of a campaign of "classical" restoration under the direction of Inigo Jones (1573–1652). The eleventh-century Norman nave and the thirteenth-century Gothic choir of the cathedral had been largely covered with stone facing in the style of the Renaissance, and the west facade had been reconstituted into a Corinthian portico. A few months before the fire, Wren had been asked to suggest further reconstruction. His report had called for rebuilding the interior to make it correspond to the Renaissance exterior, and for replacing the pointed medieval vaulting with lighter, domical vaults. In the course of his survey of old St. Paul's, Wren had found fault with what he termed its "Saracen" (meaning Gothic to Wren) style of building. He had observed that the piers were visibly out of plumb as a result of shoddy building, and he had condemned the use of flying buttresses exposed to the weather.[18] He had also proposed to replace the central tower with a dome topped by a spire.

The most interesting structural feature of Wren's early scheme for St. Paul's was the light, high outer dome, which was to be constructed of timber and supported by an inner masonry shell. The concept of this type of domical structure may have come directly from the much smaller dome of the Church of the Sorbonne in Paris, built some 30 years before by Jacques Lemercier (ca. 1582–1654) and generally assumed by Wren's biographers to have been observed by him (on his only known trip abroad) in 1665. As a matter of fact, this type of double-shell partial timber construction can be traced back through a sequence of buildings—including Sta. Maria della Salute, designed in 1630 by the Venetian architect Baldassare Longhena (1598–1682)—to medieval Venice, where it was used in the thirteenth-century enlargement of the high domes of St. Mark's Cathedral.

After the London fire, when it was eventually agreed that the old St. Paul's Cathedral could not be salvaged, Wren evidently considered himself free to draw on Roman precedent for a new design, as he had done for the Sheldonian Theater. But the ease with which he had broken with architectural tradition at Oxford was not to be repeated with his ecclesiastical clients in London. Even with the backing of Charles II, he could not prevail against the insistence of the high-church clergy that the layout of the new building follow "cathedral fashion"—that it have the cruciform plan of a medieval church, as had the old St. Paul's (figure 5.7a). This issue, probably more than any other, required Wren to produce and submit a series of designs and to make major concessions to the ecclesiastical authorities (and to popular taste) before work on the new St. Paul's finally began in 1675.

What Wren initially had in mind for the cathedral can be surmised from two city plans that he produced soon after the fire. Both indicate a structure reminiscent of the Roman Pantheon and consisting principally of a domed rotunda joined to a rectangular hall.[19] Some commentators have dismissed these plans as merely casual sketches. Nonetheless, they already convey Wren's unshakable determination to produce a domical structure and his reluctance to follow the traditional cruciform plan. Moreover, these early designs may reflect his Protestantism, insofar as they drew the entire congregation into a more proximate assemblage than was possible in the subdivided, screened, and chanceled medieval church.

Wren had a high regard for the liturgy of the English prayer book, and he conceived of a church as an "auditory" where the

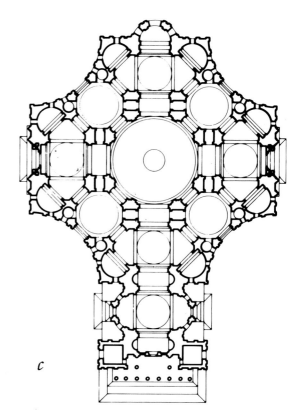

c

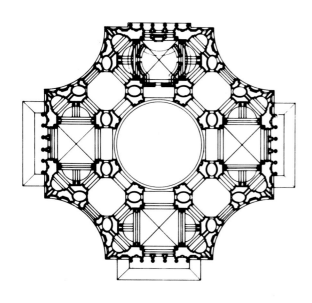

b

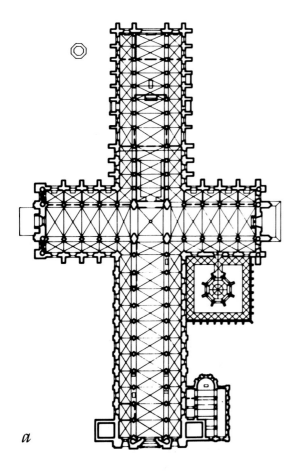

a

d

5.7

*Comparative plans: (a) Old Saint
Paul's Cathedral; (b) Greek Cross
design; (c) Great Model design;
(d) Wren's Saint Paul's Cathedral.*

congregation would hear as well as see the preacher. He estimated
the maximum distance a preacher's voice might carry, and he designed his churches accordingly. The Protestant expectation that
the clergy and the laity would participate jointly in the service
called for a compact meeting room uncluttered by screens. The
city-plan sketches, with a domed rotunda for ceremonial occasions
and a simple, rectangular hall for ordinary services, were evidently
designed to meet the ecclesiastical requirements of English Protestantism. Indeed, the city-plan designs may not be casual sketches;
they may reflect strongly held ideas about the form appropriate to
a Protestant cathedral.

The influence of Protestantism can also be seen in Wren's
designs for parish churches. "It would be vain," he wrote, "to
make a Parish church larger than that all who are present can both
hear and see."[20] In designing the parish church of St. James, Wren
tried to build the ideal auditorium, with the nave and the chancel
in a single room and with balconies to increase the seating capacity without enlarging the hall: "I can hardly think it practicable to
make a single Room so capacious, with Pews and Galleries, as to
hold 2,000 Persons, and all to hear the Service, and both to hear
distinctly, and see the Preacher. I endeavoured to effect this in
building the Parish Church of St. James's, Westminster, which I
presume is the most capacious, with these Qualifications, that hath
yet been built."[21]

The city-plan sketches of St. Paul's Cathedral were forerun-
ners of the next series of designs, on which Wren began to work
in earnest in 1670. These, too, were based on a structure whose
chief space was domed and circular. One version, the "Greek
Cross Design" (figure 5.7b), incorporated a great raised central
dome that resembles a plan for St. Peter's in Rome proposed by
Donato Bramante (1444–1514) in the early sixteenth century.
Bramante's plan, like Wren's, was rejected by clergy who remained
committed to the cruciform configuration.

In 1673, in an attempt to mollify his critics, Wren offered
what turned out to be the last of this central-plan series: the
"Great Model Design," whose plan was similar to the Greek Cross
Design except for a grudgingly introduced elongation along the
east-west axis to form a short nave and a rudimentary choir
(figure 5.7c). The large wooden model constructed to exhibit this
design (hence the origin of its title) is still extant in the cathedral's
Trophy Room (figure 5.8). It was built on a raised base with its
floor elevation scaled to eye level so that the interior is perceived

5.8

Christopher Wren: the Great Model, 1673.

5.9

Christopher Wren: Warrant Design for St. Paul's Cathedral, 1674.

by a viewer as it would appear in the completed building. In producing the model, Wren went to considerable trouble and expense to impress his patrons with what he considered to be a satisfcatory compromise. To his chagrin, the effort did not succeed, and he resolved "to make no more Models, or to publicly expose [his] Drawings."[22]

Wren's next effort, the awkward "Warrant Design" of 1674 (figure 5.9), has been interpreted as an exasperated and contemptuous reply to his critics.[23] It represented a retrogression almost to the old St. Paul's as modified by Inigo Jones. The drawings of the Warrant Design are known to have been prepared in some haste, which suggests that Wren drew upon preexisting designs. Wren's biographers cite as sources a number of earlier buildings described in sixteenth- and seventeenth-century architectural literature; it is also possible that this is one of Wren's own early designs, rehabilitated from his file. In any event, the design served Wren's immediate purpose. Charles II signed the warrant allowing construction to begin with the understanding that Wren would be free to make certain alterations. Wren evidently interpreted his freedom quite broadly; it seems to have been his intention from the outset to use the warrant as a cover under which he could restore many of the elements of his earlier plans.

In the cathedral as it finally materialized, Wren effectively created two buildings. The interior (figure 5.10)—which is modeled on a medieval basilican plan (compare figures 5.7a and 5.7d) and elevation, with a high center aisle flanked by lower side aisles— even incorporates flying buttresses intended to support the clerestory walls (figure 5.11). Nothing of this form, however, is sug-

5.10
Christopher Wren: St. Paul's Cathedral, London, (1675–1710): interior, looking east.

5.11
St. Paul's Cathedral: flying buttresses of the choir.

5.12
St. Paul's Cathedral: view from the southeast.

5.13
Comparative cross-sections of the choir of old Saint Paul's Cathedral (left) and Wren's choir.

gested to a viewer on the street, to whom the great central dome appears to rise from a massive two-story base. (The top of the cross illustrated in figure 5.12 is 112 m [366 ft] above ground level.) The cross-section (figure 5.13) reveals that this effect was achieved by raising the perimeter walls so that they conceal both the inner features of the building and the flying buttresses—an arrangement that led to charges of architectural fraud. The walls, replete with false "windows," are nothing more than "screens" calculated to hide the Gothic clerestory and flying buttresses of which Wren disapproved. Yet the extremely heavy section of these walls has also given rise to the thought that they were in fact intended to play a structural role, perhaps to resist the thrust of the flying buttresses or to help support the dome.

Somers Clark, who had been Surveyor of the Fabric of St. Paul's from 1896 to 1906, sprang to Wren's defense in 1923. Clark rationalized the "screen" walls as "buttress" walls, arguing

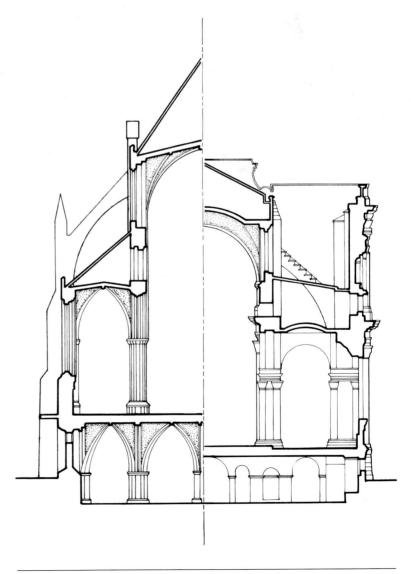

*Photoelastic interference pattern in
model of the structure of Wren's choir
under simulated dead-weight loading.*

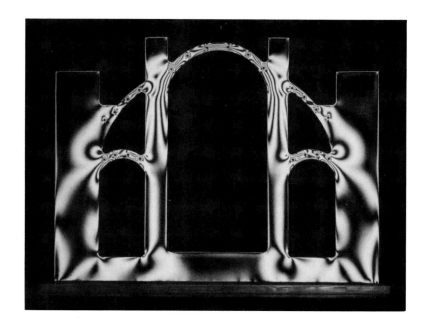

that they not only stabilize the great bastions that receive the
thrust of the arches which support the dome but also serve as buttresses "to receive the thrusts of the aisle vaults and of the flying
buttresses which maintain the high vaults."[24] To confront the
question of Wren's purposes, with an eye toward the possibility
that he employed scientific insights, we analyzed the structure
of a typical bay of St. Paul's, using photoelastic modeling in the
same manner in which it was used to study Gothic structures
(chapter 4).

The model was first tested under simulated loadings scaled
to actual dead weight (figure 5.14); then a second test was performed by applying scaled wind loadings, determined as in chapter 2. After the first series of tests was completed, the flying
buttresses were removed from the model and it was tested again
under the scaled dead-weight and wind loads. Without the flying
buttresses, stresses in the piers were higher, but it was ascertained
that well-constructed piers of solid masonry (or at least piers having a firm outer shell composed of several layers of coursed masonry) could successfully resist both the thrusts of the vaulting
and the effects of high winds. Evidently, Wren's flying buttresses
were unnecessary.

In view of Wren's earlier warning that flying buttresses "are the first thing that occasion the ruin of Cathedrals," it is especially ironic that he employed them in St. Paul's. Of course, Wren may have believed that both the flyers and the heavy perimeter walls are necessary for the building's structural integrity. Nevertheless, even this defense of the walls is questionable. If Wren was thinking only of structural necessity, he could have provided discrete piers placed to receive each flying buttress but still hidden behind light continuous walls along the perimeter of the cathedral. In response to Somers Clark's suggestion that the perimeter walls also buttress the side-aisle vaults, it should be noted that the thrust of these vaults reaches the walls (which have an overall height of 31 m [102 ft]) at a low level. Even allowing that Wren considered the additional height (and, hence, the additional weight) to increase stability, the height to which he carried these massive and expensive walls suggests that he was using them primarily for visual effect.

To deal with Clark's further assertion that the perimeter walls help to stabilize the four bastions at the crossing, which form part of the buttressing of the great dome, we performed a separate finite-element modeling of the dome. But before assessing Wren's dome design, we must review the experience of his age with earlier great domes.

Great Renaissance Domes

Structural innovation was not an outstanding characteristic of the architecture of the Renaissance. Indeed, the very word Renaissance implies a deliberate revival of the styles of classical antiquity. Moreover, the widespread publication of drawings and plans of both ancient and contemporary buildings, a new development of that era, seems to have inspired more emulation than experimentation.[25] Yet because of their huge scale, which appears related to the "rediscovery" of the Pantheon in Rome, great Renaissance domes were the principal exception.

The first of these domes came to fruition as a project to complete a giant Gothic church that had been in construction since 1294 in Florence, the Cathedral of Santa Maria. The octagonal opening of the supporting drum to be covered by the dome was 42 m (138 ft) across the dome base (between flats) and about 55 m (180 ft) above ground level, a scale that all but ruled out the possibility of erecting the dome on timber centering supported

from the floor below. The principal architect, and (perhaps even more important in this instance) also the *builder* of the dome project that began in 1420, was Filippo Brunelleschi. He overcame the formidable problem of how to support the rising dome by constructing a pointed, intricately ribbed, double-shell brick-and-stone dome of enormous total thickness (tapering slightly from about 4 m overall at its base) in horizontal full-ring layers to maintain stability.[26] Timber centering was then used to erect the fabric of the more horizontal upper portions of the dome, where the spans from side to side were appreciably less than that across the supporting drum below. A great timber chain and iron-clamped sandstone blocks encircle the dome to help resist outward thrusts. The final stage of construction—the placement of the heavy stone central lantern—was completed by 1462, 16 years after the death of the designer. Brunelleschi's dome (figure 5.15) was considered the most magnificent technological and artistic feat of the age, but it was not entirely free of structural problems. Similar problems became evident in the giant dome of St. Peter's Basilica in Rome, whose construction was begun almost half a century after the completion of the Florence cathedral. And the Roman basilica seems to have had a much more direct influence on Wren's design for St. Paul's.

Although there are some parallels between St. Paul's and St. Peter's (for example, the need to demolish earlier, tottering monuments occupying the sites), the contrasts between these two major church building projects are most significant. Instead of the single architect of St. Paul's, no fewer than eleven architects were in charge of the various stages of the erection of St. Peter's, extending from 1506 until 1667—and among them were the premier artists of the Italian Renaissance, who were certain to leave the marks of their own individuality.[27] Under the direction of Bramante, the first principal architect, construction was begun on the four massive piers that were to support the high central dome. Although Bramante apparently made no detailed design for the dome itself (Bramante's successors concluded that his piers were not massive enough to support the dome, and had them reinforced), it was his piers that set the clear diameter for the dome at 42 meters (138 feet). As at Florence, the span of St. Peter's is but one meter less than that of the Pantheon, which again points strongly to the influence of that ancient building.

It was left for Michelangelo to plan and to begin the construction of the dome of St. Peter's (between 1546 and 1564), and it was completed in somewhat different form between 1588 and 1593 by Giacomo della Porta (1533–1602) with the assistance of the "engineer" Domenico Fontana (who is better known for having reerected the Egyptian obelisk in the Piazza di San Pietro in 1586). The dome (figure 5.16) also incorporates a thick, ribbed double shell of brick and stone, which enhances its stability and reduces the height of the interior profile so that the underside of the dome does not appear to be at the end of a long, darkened cylinder (figure 5.17). A massive stone lantern was also place above the summit of the St. Peter's dome (figure 5.18).

Even though their profiles are pointed (that of Florence more so than that of St. Peter's), which serves to reduce thrusts somewhat, both domes, which must also provide support for the heavy central lanterns, are plagued with structural problems for not being adequately buttressed.[28] The primary cause of the problem becomes evident when we compare the cross-section through the dome of St. Peter's and its supporting structure with that of the Pantheon (figure 5.16). In the ancient building, the dome's outer profile is relatively flat, and buttressing against the outward thrusts of the dome is well provided for by the massive cylindrical concrete wall. At St. Peter's, even greater outward thrusts are exerted by the dome, but there is only the vertical portion of the relatively thin cylindrical drum below the dome to provide what has proved to be inadequate resistance. Two iron chains were placed around the base of the dome by della Porta to help prevent its spreading; but the problem is aggravated by the great weight of the dome, which generates extremely large outward forces. Almost from the beginning the dome began to crack along meridians as it spread outward, and five more chains were added by the middle of the eighteenth century.[29]

Although the diameter of Wren's dome for St. Paul's, 31 meters (101 feet), was to be only three-quarters that of St. Peter's, Wren seems to have been alarmed by reports of problems with the Roman Basilica. His close friend and fellow member of the Royal Society John Evelyn (1620–1706) had examined St. Peter's and probably provided Wren with a firsthand account of its structural problems. Evelyn had a keen interest in architecture, and his reports may have contributed to Wren's hesitation in making a final choice of a dome design from among many schemes that he worked on almost until the construction of the dome was undertaken (between 1705 and 1708). It can be assumed that Wren's starting point for the structural design of the new St. Paul's dome

Comparative cross-sections: St. Peter's
Basilica (left); Pantheon, Rome (right).

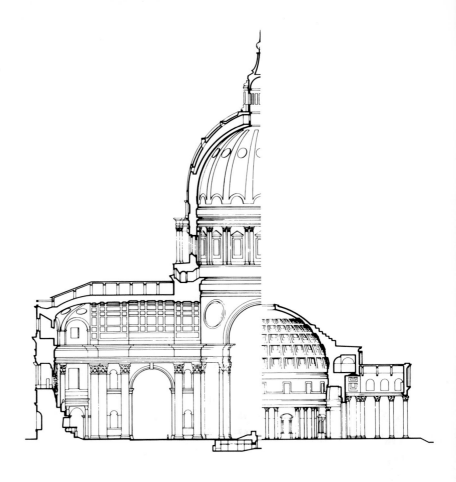

5.17
Interior of the dome of St. Peter's
Basilica, illuminated by light from cen-
tral lantern.

5.18
Giacomo della Porta: dome of St. Peter's
Basilica, 1588–1593.

was the double-shell dome scheme he had proposed for the old
cathedral. In addition to the variations that he worked on in his
proposals for the new St. Paul's, Wren designed and built a large
timber-domed parish church in London—St. Stephen's Wal-
brook—between 1672 and 1679. But because the dome of St.
Stephen's was wholly of timber, the experience would not have
been particularly helpful to him in arriving at a solution for St.
Paul's. We know that Wren continued to worry over the problem.
As late as 1694 there are several references in his notes to experimental dome models, and some dome sketches made under his
direction and dated as late as 1703 are not yet the final version.[30]

Wren also faced problems of another kind. Just as Bramante
had done at St. Peter's, Wren began the construction of the crossing piers well before the dome design was in hand. But instead of
the four massive piers of the Roman basilica, Wren placed eight

piers in line with the piers of the arcades (illustrated in figure 5.7d) and then added the bastions—the four heavy tower-like structures at the reentrant corners of the transepts—which provide more stability to the dome. All these structures were then joined together by an array of arches and barrel vaulting, so that no light is admitted to the bays immediately adjacent to the domed space.[31] Building records indicate problems with spalling of the rubble-filled piers as early as 1690, and differential settlement of the central piers was observed from 1696 on.[32] These concerns may well have prompted Wren to adopt the extremely lightweight design illustrated in figure 5.19—a truly elegant solution both artistically and technologically.

Wren's design is based on a majestic, light outer dome profile of lead-sheathed timber supported by an unseen chain-girdled brick cone, only 46 centimeters (18 inches) thick, which also supports a stone lantern of some 850 tons, and a separate brick dome (also 46 cm thick) which, seen from the interior, produces an effect strikingly like that of the interior dome of St. Peter's (compare figures 5.17 and 5.20). In contrast to the action of the dome of St. Peter's, though, the brick cone of St. Paul's, formed by straight-line generators, is compressed by the heavy central lantern. Hence the cone, which also provides almost all of the support for the outer, visible dome, experiences compression throughout rather than the pernicious tension characteristic of heavy spherical domes.[33]

In further contrast to St. Peter's, Wren's single iron chain proved sufficient to maintain the integrity of his relatively light structure against outward thrusts. Our model study of the triple-dome configuration indicated that stresses within the supporting masonry are generally low under both gravity and wind forces, and that the single chain is well placed to fulfill its role. There have been problems with the dome's supporting structure, as mentioned above, but these are not related to the structure of the dome itself. In fact, had Wren arrived at this final dome design at an earlier stage of the project, before beginning the construction of the central supporting piers, he might well have perceived that the piers could have been lightened, and some of the distress resulting from their settlement would thus have been avoided.

The triumph of Wren's solution is borne out by the fact that St. Peter's turned out to be the last of the great domes to be constructed entirely in masonry. Wren's structural scheme for the dome of St. Paul's became the standard for all the large dome

Section through St. Paul's Cathedral, showing Wren's structural solution for the dome (J. Gwyn, 1753).

projects that followed St. Paul's, well into the nineteenth century—including the dome over the U.S. Capitol Building (constructed by Thomas U. Walter between 1856 and 1864), which is similar in scale. Even so, Wren's design hardly required theoretical analysis to make it work; nor for that matter did our modeling give any indication that the heavy, raised perimeter walls play any role in helping to stabilize the dome.

If Wren failed to achieve the elusive merger of theory and practice in his architecture, it was not through lack of purpose. In several commentaries and in the fragmentary tracts his son and grandson compiled in the *Parentalia*, Wren asserted unambiguously that the science of statics must form the basis of building. In 1713 he summed up his attitude in a report on Westminster Abbey: "It is by due Consideration of the Statick Principles, and the right Poising of the Weights of the Butments to Arches, that good Architecture depends."[34] Indeed, he went beyond this programmatic

5.20

Interior of the dome of St. Paul's Cathedral. Note similarities with St. Peter's in form and illumination.

endorsement and made the practical suggestion that where a column cannot be made stout enough to resist the horizontal thrust of an arch, its resistance can be increased by making it taller and hence heavier.

Wren's views on the place of theoretical mechanics in architecture, and on the priority of the utilitarian over the ornamental, are set out most clearly in his *Tract II*, an undated, fragmentary treatise that begins with a discussion of the five classical orders of column design (designated Doric, Ionic, Corinthian, Tuscan, and Composite). They had been reduced, he wrote, to "Rules, too strict and pedantick, and so as not to be transgressed, without the Crime of Barbarity; though in their own Nature, they are but the Modes and Fashions of those Ages wherein they were used."[35]

Wren turned next in *Tract II* to an analysis of the arch:

It seems very unaccountable that the Generality of our late Architects dwell so much upon this ornamental, and so slightly pass over the geometrical, which is the most essential Part of Architecture. For Instance, can an Arch stand without Butment sufficient? If the Butment be more than enough, 'tis an idle Expense of Materials; if too little, it will fall; and so for any Vaulting: And yet no Author hath given a true and universal Rule for this; nor hath considered all the various Forms of Arches.

Wren concluded that the "true and universal Rule" can be deduced only from the science of mechanics. "What is true," he wrote, "will be shown to be only determinable by the Doctrine of finding the Centers of Gravity in the Parts of the proposed Design." Although the rule that Wren formulated from considering only the placement of the centers of gravity is incorrect because it neglects (among other things) the ubiquitous *horizontal* thrust of an arch, his analysis was a response, in terms of the science of mechanics, to the foremost structural problem of the time.

It is only anachronism that has led some to believe that Wren's interest in both science and architecture must have resulted in the successful application of theoretical principles to the solution of building problems.[36] He belonged to the seventeenth century, with its flourishing of the sciences and its practical, enterprising spirit. Ironically, Wren came closest to applied science not in his actual building, but rather in his speculative tracts and his abbreviated notes.

6

The Technological Legacy
of Historic Architecture

These technical studies, spanning almost two millennia of construction, have helped to illuminate the techniques used by early builders to achieve remarkable success with large-scale structures. Although primary geometric forms—particularly those that could be simply laid out by using common instruments, such as a straight edge and a compass—were used extensively in conceptual design, they were always modified as needed for structural stability. For example, when used as a primary support, the haunches of the characteristic Roman semicircular arch were filled with cut stone, as illustrated in figure 3.1. Similarly, though the interior space of the Roman Pantheon is bounded by a primary hemispherical form, the dome extrados (including the requisite step rings) presents a much flatter, more complex profile. Confidence that a new building form would resist collapse could never have been gained from using only simple geometric rules, and other sources of the early builder's structural knowledge needed to be identified.

The studies revealed, first, that building technology follows an evolutionary pattern: Practical *experience* with earlier buildings substituted for much of the information about building performance that would be available today from numerical modeling. In effect, an earlier building served as a "model" for a new design. This process is most evident in Gothic structural development (see figure 4.2), but it was also evident in such "breakthrough" designs as the Pantheon and the Hagia Sophia. Although the span of the Pantheon's dome is about twice that of known earlier domed baths, all the techniques of Roman construction were well in place by the time of its construction. And nothing in the Hagia Sophia's history implies that its designers possessed any greater understanding of structure than might have been available through experience with buildings of the Pantheon type and from other open-walled large-domed buildings, such as the Minerva Medica in Rome (ca. A.D. 310) and SS. Sergius and Bacchus in Constantinople (completed before A.D. 536). Christopher Wren's design for the dome of St. Paul's also owed much to earlier dome projects, going back as far as the thirteenth-century reconstruction of St. Mark's in Venice. And for that matter, the illustrations of modern engineering cited by Le Corbusier—including Eiffel's Garabit Viaduct (figure 6.1), ships, airplanes, and automobiles—owed every bit as much of their design to empirical observation as to theoretical analysis.[1]

The technological elegance of many of the early structural solutions led me to discern a second factor contributing to their successes. During construction, the master builders used a technique that, although it is available to today's designers, is rarely used because of the usual separation of the modern design office from the building site, and oftentimes, too, because of a misplaced confidence in theoretical methods of analysis. This technique involved detailed observation by the builder of undesirable behavior—particularly cracking in the fabric of the building—that might occur during the process of construction. The steps then taken to eliminate these shortcomings led to refinements in design. In a sense, this approach is the forerunner of modern experimental analysis of full-scale structures, which is often performed with electric strain gauges as described in chapter 2.

A third contributing factor is the forgiving nature of typical masonry construction as compared with the relatively "high-strung" nature of slender modern structural elements of reinforced concrete and steel. Small changes in the geometry of masonry have far less effect on stability than similar changes in modern construction; and even though masonry is very weak in tension, the presence of highly localized tensions (such as that found at the ends of the original Notre-Dame flying buttresses) rarely produces a catastrophic collapse.

6.1
*Gustave Eiffel: Garabit Viaduct, Massif
Central, France, 1884.*

All of the investigations, from the ancient era through the Renaissance, point also to the fact that master builders took a keen interest in minimizing the costs of construction, including the expenses of obtaining and transporting materials as well as those of shaping and erection. Roman concrete, which could be "manufactured" at the construction site using a plentiful supply of relatively unskilled slave labor, was less expensive than cut stone brought from a quarry. The Gothic designers seem to have appreciated the technical advantages of reducing structural weight (which diminished internal forces in all the supporting members and the foundations); in turn, this expedient helped to reduce the costs of hired professional manpower, building materials, transportation of materials, and the entire erection process. The technological elegance of Wren's design for the dome of St. Paul's derives from similar considerations; but since Wren's structure was hidden behind an external dome, late-nineteenth-century and early-twentieth-century architectural theorists characterized it as immoral and even suggested that the outer covering of timber be removed to reveal the "structurally honest" load-carrying cone within.[2] Criticism of this nature lays bare the absurdity of carrying the theme of "architectural morality" to its logical end. The Renaissance high dome is, after all, primarily a work of monumental sculpture. And Wren's dome, which is even more effective visually than Michalengelo's, is far more innovative in its structural design. This rationale seems to have been perfectly clear to Gustav Eiffel, who in 1883 designed an efficient wrought-iron pylon (figure 6.2) to support the large-scale sculptural form of the Statue of Liberty in the harsh environment of New York Harbor.[3]

These studies also indicate the general concurrence of structural and stylistic experimentation in large-scale building. The introduction of new structural devices (such as the flying buttress) in the Gothic cathedral had a profound stylistic effect. And even the more sculptural Greek classical style was altered in the temple of Zeus Olympia at Agrigento to meet the demands of building on a colossal scale.[4] From all these findings it is clear that discerning the technological intentions of early designer-builders is just as important for historical study as understanding any other facet of building design—an observation humorously underscored in a cartoon by Jules Feiffer depicting a future archaeologist commenting on the architecture of our own time (figure 6.3). The time-scale determination of Feiffer's archaeologist is based entirely on

6.2
Gustave Eiffel: Statue of Liberty Pylon,
1884.

style (which seems to go hand in hand with his clothing, his projection screen, and even his pointer, all suggesting a less technological civilization than our own). The cartoon's humor derives largely from the archaeologist's failure to account for the necessarily far more advanced technology of the high-rise building—its light but rigid structure, electric lighting, modern plumbing, and high-speed elevators—all of which the brownstone can forgo. Yet there is an additional note of irony in the cartoon: Although it was first published in 1961, more than a decade before the advent of the "postmodern movement," the revelation of Feiffer's archaeologist may still prove prophetic of an architecture resulting from the contemporary artist-architect's being relieved of the burden of dealing with technical issues, as discussed in chapter 1.

OUR FIRST SLIDE SHOWS A RECONSTRUCTION OF THE EARLIEST AND MOST **PRIMITIVE** FORM OF THAT PERIOD — THE **GLASS SLAB** — BUILT PROBABLY IN THE MIDDLE NINETEENTH CENTURY. NOTICE ITS **VACUOUSNESS** AND LACK OF SCALE.

NEXT WE HAVE A **LATER**, MORE **TRANSITIONAL** HOUSE OF THE EARLY TWENTIETH CENTURY — **STILL** RATHER MONOTONOUS BUT FEATURING GREATER SOPHISTICATION OF **DETAIL**. THE RECORDS WE FOUND PROVE THAT THESE CONSTRUCTIONS WERE AT FIRST KNOWN AS "**HOUSING PROJECTS**" A CLUMSY TERM LATER SIMPLIFIED INTO "SLUMS."

OUR **LAST** SLIDE REPRESENTS A **HIGH** POINT OF PROGRESS. BUILT IN THE LATE TWENTIETH OR EARLY TWENTY-FIRST CENTURY THIS BUILDING KNOWN AS A "**BROWNSTONE**" UTILIZES A TASTE AND A FLAIR FOR EXPERIMENTATION THAT SUGGEST AN ARCHITECTURAL RENAISSANCE.

ONE CAN ONLY BE LEFT BREATHLESS BY THE BRILLIANCE OF A SOCIETY THAT WAS ABLE TO MAKE SUCH GIANT STRIDES IN A MERE ONE-HUNDRED FIFTY YEARS.

6.3

Excerpt from cartoon by Jules Feiffer

(©), 1961.

The idea that architecture (which by dictionary definition includes design *and construction*) has an "autonomous aesthetic dimension" flies in the face of inferences drawn from technology-oriented studies of past building. It also represents an opposite pole from the theory advanced by the giant of nineteenth-century historians of building technology (and the restorer of many of the major Gothic buildings cited in chapter 4), Eugène-Emmanuel Viollet-le-Duc (1814–1879). From closely observing the details of construction of numerous early buildings, Viollet-le-Duc became convinced that many of their principal stylistic elements were originally derived from the demands of the construction process or the physical laws governing structural forces.[5] And since these laws apply to all building at all times, he argued, authentic innovation in visual form springs from an appropriate response to structural demands in terms of the materials of construction. Viollet-le-Duc then attempted to demonstrate through new design proposals how the recently introduced metals of his own age might be used in the same way to develop a modern style of building (one example is illustrated in figure 6.4). To our late-twentieth-century taste these designs may not appear especially attractive or persuasive, but in their time they seem to have been a powerful influence for the general acceptance of new structural forms in iron by the French public.[6] Viollet-le-Duc's polemical writings on structural rationalism, on the other hand, have an up-to-date air about them. Consider the following excerpt:

A locomotive . . . has its peculiar physiognomy, not the result of caprice, but of necessity. It expresses controlled power; its movements are gentle or terrible, it advances with awful impetuosity or, when at rest, seems to tremble with impatience. . . . its exterior form is but the expression of its power. A locomotive, then, has style. . . . A thing has style when it has the expression appropriate to its use. . . . We, who in the fabrication of our machinery, give to every part the strength and the form which it requires, with nothing superfluous, nothing which does not have a necessary function, in our architecture foolishly accumulate forms and features taken from all sides, the results of contradictory principles, and call this art.[7]

These and many similar observations had enormous influence on the course of architectural development well into the twentieth century, in America as well as in Europe. They led the historian John Summerson, despite his own stylistic skepticism, to characterize Viollet-le-Duc as "the last great theorist in the world of architecture."[8] It is matter of record that Viollet-le-Duc's theories, which were rather quickly translated into English as the two-

volume *Discourses,* were heatedly discussed by the major designers of the late-nineteenth-century "Chicago School." He has even been credited with seeding the idea of the metal-frame American skyscraper.[9] Yet there were always commentators who were appalled by the idea that architectural style could arise primarily from technological considerations. And seemingly, as part of the general repudiation of the technological positivism that prevailed before the First World War,[10] the movement away from structural rationalism and toward the type of formalism advocated by Le Corbusier picked up momentum in the 1920s. Even so, some well-known twentieth-century designers, most of them having backgrounds in engineering as well as in architecture, continued to work in the tradition of Viollet-le-Duc's structural rationalism. These include Robert Maillart (1872–1940), Pier Luigi Nervi (1891–1979), and Fazlur Khan (1930–1982).[11]

For example, compare, the concept of the John Hancock Center in Chicago (by Skidmore, Owings & Merrill, with Fazlur Khan as structural designer) with that of the Hancock Tower in Boston (described in chapter 1). In its robust display of effective structure, the John Hancock Center comes close to the modern ideal of structural rationalism. The primary support for the vertical, dead-weight loadings and the lateral support against the wind (and possible earthquake) loadings on this 337 m (1,105 ft) tall building derive from great tapered vertical trusses placed around the exterior walls—an arrangement not unlike that of the High Gothic cathedral, with its major supporting buttresses disposed around the perimeter of the central vessel. Indeed, because of its giant scale, its unusually light structure, and the openness of its base, this landmark building might well be characterized as the Bourges Cathedral of our time.[12]

Functioning as an integrated three-dimensional "box" with all four sides participating in its support, the structure of the Hancock Center is unusually efficient. In a comparison made in 1973 of the quantity of steel used in various tall buildings (figure 6.7), the Hancock Center was shown to contain about the same weight of steel per square foot of floor area as a conventionally constructed building of just half its height.[13] As with all extremely tall buildings, its upper floors sway noticeably in high winds.[14] Even so, this has not required expensive modifications such as those made to the Hancock Tower in Boston, nor does it seem to have discouraged prospective tenants from adding their names to a long waiting list for the upper-floor apartments.

6.6

*Skidmore, Owings & Merrill: John
Hancock Center, Chicago, 1970.*

6.7

*Comparative weight of steel in tall mod-
ern buildings (after Picardi).*

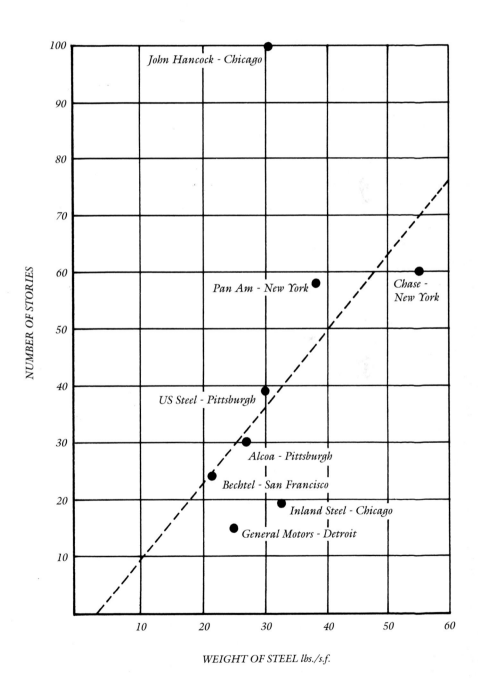

John Hancock - Chicago

Pan Am - New York

*Chase -
New York*

US Steel - Pittsburgh

Alcoa - Pittsburgh

Bechtel - San Francisco

Inland Steel - Chicago

General Motors - Detroit

NUMBER OF STORIES

WEIGHT OF STEEL lbs./s.f.

Despite its general success, I am not aware that any major design award has been conferred on the John Hancock Center (like the one conferred on the Hancock Tower in Boston by the American Institute of Architects). Nor does an award seem to be in order if we consider only a more typical, formally based précis of its design:

Two aspects of Mies's skyscraper style were seized upon and exaggerated: the sculptural weight of the fluting and the visible display of structure. . . . Skidmore, Owings & Merrill moved from designing small-scaled delicate structures, such as Lever House, to progressively heavier, even overpowering towers . . . [including] the leviathan of 1960s skyscrapers—the tapered ninety-five story John Hancock Center in Chicago, which superimposes on its dense, brawny frame a series of disruptive [*sic*] X-braces, subverting what was left of the spirit of Mies.[15]

Formal criticism without a technological dimension clearly has limitations, particularly when it is used for the analysis of large-scale projects.

I would hope that by adding a component of technological appraisal, our future archaeologist will be able to discern a "personal style" in another high-rise design design by Khan: the Marine Midland Bank Building in Rochester, New York, completed in 1968 (figure 6.8). Here, Khan has responded to the natural flow of forces in a supporting wall by introducing visually subtle but structurally significant variations in column section: higher density toward the building's lower portion, where forces from both gravity and wind action are greater, and even an expression with the vertical columns of the (nonvertical) arching action above the piers at the building's base.

If we desire more rational technology in contemporary building design, our architectural criticism will have to employ the type of scrutiny that is being increasingly used in studies of historic buildings. It is not my intent to insist, along the lines of Viollet-le-Duc, that all great architecture necessarily comes from technological exigencies. But I do hold that *appropriate* structure should always be used for large-scale buildings. I include in this category projects created primarily for visual effect, even when this leads to a literal separation of the supporting structure from the sculptural form (as in Wren's design for the dome of St. Paul's Cathedral). Although one tends to admire a style whose development coincides with structural necessity, forcing this coincidence, as did the designers of the Sydney Opera House, is neither good engineering nor good architecture.

Notes

Chapter 1

1

Engineering News Record, April 5, 1973, p. 13.

2

O. N. Arup and G. J. Kunz, "Sydney Opera House," *Civil Engineering* 41 (December 1971): 50.

3

On the issue of tension between technology and art, see Sigfried Giedion, *Space, Time, and Architecture,* fifth edition (Harvard University Press, 1967), p. 676ff. Giedion considers that any opposition to the Opera House project simply "gives rise to a basic question. A question that our period must again answer and decide, a question of consequence. Are we prepared to go beyond the purely functional and tangible as earlier periods did in order to enhance the force of expression?" He is insensitive to the issue of "honest" vs. logical, hidden structure, and in fact his argument is not dissimilar to Arup's (note 2 above).

4

Allan Temko, *Eero Saarinen* (Braziller, 1962), pp. 28–29; Aline Saarinen, ed., *Eero Saarinen and his Work* (Yale University Press, 1962), p. 151.

5

By definition, the three sides of a *spherical triangle* are composed of great circles. Hence, each of the sides of a right equilateral spherical triangle must subtend a solid angle (at the center of the sphere) of 90°; the total surface of the sphere is thus made up of eight equilateral spherical triangles.

6

Engineering News Record, May 26, 1977, p. 16. Not all observers agree about the Hancock Tower's visual quality: ". . . such a cool, mirror-glass building . . . is as forbidding, antisocial, and hostile as a person wearing mirror sunglasses. Ask it what it is or where to enter, and it tells you that the sky is blue and that you are on the sidewalk." (Marvin Trachtenberg and Isabelle Hyman, *Architecture: From Pre-history to Modernism* [Prentice-Hall/Abrams, 1986], p. 546)

7

On recent architectural publishing, see Robert Gutman, *Architectural Practice: A Critical View* (Princeton Architectural Press, 1988), p. 92ff.

8

Alberto Pérez-Gómez, *Architecture and the Crisis of Modern Science* (MIT Press, 1983), pp. 314–315.

9

Ibid., p. 161.

10

See, e.g., William L. Macdonald, *The Architecture of the Roman Empire,* volume 1, revised edition (Yale University Press, 1982), pp. 143–154.

11

Joseph Giovannini, "The Grand Reach of Corporate America," *New York Times,* January 20, 1985. Office buildings cited in the article include the AT&T headquarters in New York (1979–1984) and the Republic Bank in Houston (1981–1984) by Johnson and Burgee, the Procter & Gamble headquarters in Cincinnati (1982–1985) by Kohn, Pederson, and Fox, and the Humana headquarters in Louisville (1980–1982) by Michael Graves.

12

Gutman, *Architectural Practice,* p. 18.

13

Ibid., pp. 38–40. The extent of this feeling of "liberation" is evident in the subtitle of a *New York Times Magazine* article on "deconstructivist" architecture that appeared at the time of this writing: "A new design sensibility is stretching the boundaries of architecture by casting doubts on basic assumptions—including gravity." (J. Giovannini, "Breaking the Rules," June 12, 1988)

14

Le Corbusier (Charles-Edouard Jeanneret), *Towards a New Architecture,* tr. F. Etchells (Praeger, 1960; originally published as *Vers Une Architecture,* Paris, 1923), p. 7. Le Corbusier's illustrations of engineering triumphs include Gustave Eiffel's Garabit Viaduct (completed in 1884) and contemporary ships, airplanes, and automobiles. Mathematical analysis was used for some aspects of their design, but the fluid dynamics of the hulls of ships and of aircraft is far too complex to have been described mathematically in 1923.

15

Le Corbusier, *Towards a New Architecture,* pp. 7, 31–33. Le Corbusier finds Gothic architecture ("not, fundamentally, based on spheres, cones, and cylinders") to be "not very beautiful." "We search in it," he writes, "for compensations of a subjective kind outside plastic art. . . . *The [Gothic] cathedral is not a plastic work: it is a drama; a fight against the force of gravity, which is a sensation of a sentimental nature.*"

16

An 1889 competition for the design of a taller tower, to be built in London, brought forth 68 proposals. The jury was disappointed by what appeared to be a problem of originality; as the jury itself pointed out, "in the Eiffel Tower the most natural and obvious way of combining economic construction and suitable architectural effect had already been appropriated." See Robert Jay, "Taller than Eiffel's Tower: The London and Chicago Tower Projects, 1889–1994," *Journal of the Society of Architectural Historians* 46 (June 1987): 146–147.

17

Reyner Banham, *A Concrete Atlantis* (MIT Press, 1986), pp. 17–18.

18

Ibid., p. 18.

19

The question of the origin of Greek monumental architecture is discussed by J. J. Coulton in *Ancient Greek Architects at Work: Problems of Structure and Design* (Cornell University Press, 1977), p. 30ff.

20

Coulton, *Ancient Greek Architects at Work*, p. 82ff. Joints between the ashlar blocks at the center of each "lintel" span of Zeus Olympia made additional vertical support appear necessary—a problem that was solved by inserting giant male figures with upraised forearms between the columns.

21

According to Coulton (*Ancient Greek Architects at Work*, pp. 123, 140), "Hellenistic architects . . . never showed the interest Roman architects had in designing impressive interiors; for them the important space was on the outside. . . . The structural conservatism [of the post-and-lintel system] is probably inherent in the Greek conception of architecture as concerned primarily with external form rather than internal space."

22

R. Mark, "Structural Experimentation in Gothic Architecture," *American Scientist* 66 (1978): 549.

23

See note 13, above.

Chapter 2

1

Stephen Jay Gould, *Ever Since Darwin: Reflections in Natural History* (Norton, 1977), pp. 175–177. In a letter to the author, dated April 14, 1987, Gould wrote that he had "convinced [himself] of the fallacy of [his] old hypothesis about light and scaling," and suggested a new explanation "that would still reside entirely in the domain of scaling, but would substitute structure for light."

2

But this illustration does not preclude the use of other types of early footings. Sheila Bonde and Clark Maines have found evidence of medieval
footings acting in the manner of modern piles to convey surface building
loads through a relatively weak soil to a stronger subsoil ("Reedificare de
Fundamentis: The State of Research on Gothic Foundation Systems,"
forthcoming). Tests of soil samples from a building site, which provide
data such as soil weight, strength, and *in situ* moisture content, can usually be used with modern theory to provide reliable footing designs (see,
e.g., Wayne C. Teng, *Foundation Design* [Prentice-Hall, 1962], pp. 57–67).
Of course, none of this theory was available to the early builders.

3

This helps to explain the disposition of a footing below a pier buttress of
Amiens Cathedral that was excavated in the nineteenth century and described by Eugéne-Emmanuel Viollet-le-Duc in the *Dictionaire raisonné de
l'architecture française du XIe au XVIe siècle,* (Librairies-Imprimeries
Réunies, 1854–1868), vol. 4, p. 175): "At the cathedral of Amiens, where
we were able to examine the foundation [down] to natural soil we found
[some 8 m (26 ft) below ground level] a layer of *terre à brique,* 40 cm
(16 in) thick set on virgin clay; at B [the letters refer to figure 100 in volume 4] a bed of concrete 40 cm thick; then, from C to D, 14 courses of
rough ashlar, each from 30 to 40 cm thick, [extracted] from the quarries
of Blavelincourt near Amiens. This stone is a very hard chalk [with inclu-
sions] filled with silica which they quarried in large pieces. Above, we
find one course, E, of Croissy stone, then 3 courses, F, of [very dense]
sandstone [just] below ground level. Above ground level, the entire
building rests on 6 other courses, G, of very hard well-dressed sandstone.
Behind the face of the foundation is a core of large fragments of flint and
stone from Blavelincourt and from Croissy, set in a very hard, well-made
mortar. It is on this artificial mountain that the immense cathedral rests."
(translation: C. Maines) A recent technical study indicates the load applied to the hard clay soil below a footing supporting an arcade pier in
the choir of Amiens Cathedral is 1,660 metric tons (1,830 tons), including
the 1,100-metric-ton (1,210-ton) self-weight of the footing. The footing
area, estimated as 70 m^2 (750 ft^2), gives an effective soil bearing pressure
of 24 metric ton/m^2 (2.4 ton/ft^2), which is surprisingly close to the modern footing design standards given in table 2.1 (S. Bonde, C. Maines, and
R. Mark, "Archaeology and Engineering: The Foundations of Amiens
Cathedral," *Kunstchronik* 42 [July 1989]: 341–348).

4

James E. Gordon, *The New Science of Strong Materials* (Princeton University Press, 1984), pp. 141–145.

5

Timber anisotropy was the main reason for specifying a model of wood,
rather than one of isotropic plastic, for the Westminster Hall study described below.

6

On the strength of early mortar, see Henri Masson, "Le rationalisme dans l'architecture du moyen age," *Bulletin Monumental* 94 (1935): 29–50.

7

Freshly quarried stone is "green" with groundwater (known as "quarry sap"), which evaporates when exposed to the atmosphere. See Robert J. Schaffer, *The Weathering of Natural Building Stones* (Garston, 1972), p. 15. Rates of absorption for bricks and building stones vary according to their natural properties and moisture content, but all absorb considerable amounts of water and set a mortar under normal circumstances. See Sven Sahlin, *Structural Masonry* (Prentice-Hall, 1971), p. 12ff.

8

Sahlin, *Structural Masonry,* pp. 52–56.

9

Henry Cowan reported on the results of modern test of concrete from ancient Roman ruins in Libya. These indicated a compressive strength of about 200 kg/cm² (2,800 psi), not far from that of modern concrete using Portland cement (*The Masterbuilders* [Wiley, 1977] p. 56). On the basis of an empirical relationship developed for modern concrete (George Winter and Arthur H. Nilson, *Design of Concrete Structures,* eighth edition [McGraw-Hill, 1972], p. 22), the theoretical tensile strength of the Libyan specimen could be as high as 15 kg/cm² (210 psi).

10

See Emil Simiu and Robert H. Scanlon, *Wind Effects on Structures,* second edition (Wiley-Interscience, 1986), pp. 162ff., 572–581. On the history of the technology used to measure wind's direction, velocity, and pressure, see W. E. Knowles Middleton, *Invention of the Meteorological Instruments* (Johns Hopkins University Press, 1969), pp. 175–230.

11

R. Mark, *Experiments in Gothic Structure* (MIT Press, 1982), p. 23.

12

Ibid., p. 24.

13

W. W. Clark and R. Mark, "The First Flying Buttresses: A New Reconstruction of the Nave of Notre-Dame de Paris, *Art Bulletin* 66 (March 1984): 47–65.

14

P. W. Bridgeman, *Dimensional Analysis* (Yale University Press, 1931). Although the operations of dimensional analysis are simple, the selection of appropriate dimensionless ratios is based on what Bridgeman (on p. 5) saw as "requiring a considerable background of physical experience and the exercise of discreet judgement. The untutored savage in the bushes would probably not be able to apply the method . . . to obtain results which would satisfy us."

15

Realizing this, Galileo commented: "It is manifest that if one wished to maintain in an enormous giant those properties of members that exist in an ordinary man, it would be necessary either to find much harder and more resistant material to form his bones, or else allow his robustness to be proportionally weaker than in men of average stature." (Galileo Galilei, *Two New Sciences,* tr. Stillman Drake [University of Wisconsin Press, 1974; Leyden: Elzevirs, 1638], p. 128). The effect of scale variations in classical Greek temples is discussed in J. J. Coulton's *Ancient Greek Architects at Work: Problems of Structure and Design* (Cornell University Press, 1977), pp. 74–96.

16

R. Mark, "Photomechanical Model Analysis of Concrete Structures," in *Models for Concrete Structures* (American Concrete Institute, 1970), pp. 187–214.

17

This phenomenon also underlies the use of models made of certain visco-elastic plastics to predict elastic response. See Raymond D. Midlin, "A Mathematical Theory of Photo-visco-elasticity," *Journal of Applied Physics* 20 (1949): 206–216.

18

See Robert D. Cook, *Concepts and Applications of Finite Element Analysis,* second edition (Wiley, 1981).

19

Lynn T. Courtenay, "The Westminster Hall Roof and its 14th-Century Sources," *Journal of the Society of Architectural Historians* 43 (December 1984): 295–309.

20

See Jacques Heyman, "Westminster Hall Roof," *Proceedings of the Institution of Civil Engineers* 37 (May 1967): 137–162; "Discussion of 'Westminster Hall Roof' by J. Heyman," ibid. 38 (September 1967): 785–796.

21

See Yun-Sheng Huang, *Westminster Hall and the Hammer-Beam Roof, A New Structural Interpretation,* Ph.D. thesis, Princeton University, 1986; Lynn T. Courtenay and R. Mark, "The Westminster Hall Roof: A Historiographic and Structural Study," *Journal of the Society Architectural Historians* 46 (December 1987): 374–393. The major source of detailed joint information is a 1914 parliamentary report by Frank Baines: *Report on Condition of the Roof Timber of Westminster Hall,* Commissioned Document 7436, House of Commons.

22

Problems with strain-gauge measurements of timber structures are discussed in Courtenay and Mark, "The Westminster Hall Roof" (note 23). These problems are hardly unique to our modeling; earlier, similar experience is reported in *Study of the Behavior of Old Frame Structures* (Ottawa: Restoration Services Division, Engineering and Architecture Branch, Department of Indian and Northern Affairs, 1976).

23

See Otto von Simson, *The Gothic Cathedral,* second edition (Harper and Row, 1962), pp. 50–58.

24

Although unmeasurable, both sound quality and light saturation can be *compared* with agreed-upon standards. See Paul J. Boylan, *Elements of Physics* (Allyn & Bacon, 1965), pp. 373–383.

25

Recommended illuminance varies from 5 foot-candles for parking garages to 500 foot-candles for minor surgery (C. Ramsey and H. Sleeper, *Architectural Graphic Standards,* sixth edition [Wiley, 1970], p. 639). These lighting standards are subject to fairly frequent revision.

Chapter 3

1

Vitruvius, *The Ten Books of Architecture,* tr. M. H. Morgan (Dover, 1960).

2

The Pantheon was consecrated by Pope Boniface IV in ca. A.D. 609. During the middle ages, it suffered from a "united belief that it owed its existence to sinister forces of demons—the familiar dense row of pillars supporting the vault in Gothic cathedrals was miraculously lacking—and not to the ratio or the genius of its architect" (T. Buddensieg, "Criticism and Praise of the Pantheon in the Middle Ages and the Renaissance," in *Classical Influences on European Culture AD* 500–1500, ed. R. R. Bolgar (Cambridge University Press, 1971).

3

William L. MacDonald, *The Pantheon: Design, Meaning and Progeny* (Harvard University Press, 1976), p. 13.

4

For background on late-nineteenth-century long-span structures, see Donald Hoffmann, "Clear Span Rivalry: The World Fairs of 1889–1893, *Journal of the Society of Architectural Historians* 29 (March 1970): 48–50. On the shell roof of the Centre National des Industries et des Techniques, see Mario Salvadori, *Why Buildings Stand Up* (McGraw-Hill 1980), pp. 242–245.

5

Suetonius, *De vita Caesarum,* tr. F. W. Rolfe, in *The Lives of the Caesars* (London: W. Heinman, 1913).

6

J. B. Ward-Perkins, *Roman Imperial Architecture* (Penguin, 1981), p. 68ff.

7

Ibid., p. 98.

8

This idea seems to have been first proposed near the close of the nineteenth century by J. Henry Middleton, Slade Professor of Fine Arts and Director of the Fitzwilliam Museum at the University of Cambridge: "It would have been impossible for the Romans to build and vault their enormous spans if they had used vaulting of brick and masonry. . . . Roman concrete was quite devoid of any lateral thrust, and covered its space with the rigidity of a metal lid. . . . The construction of the enormous cupola is . . . as free from thrusts as if it were cut out of one block of stone." (*The Remains of Ancient Rome* [London: Adam & Charles Black, 1892] pp. I-66 and II-131)

9

J.-H. Prévost, Dyna-Flow User's Manual, Department of Civil Engineering, Princeton University, 1983.

10

The actual structure of the wall, which also incorporates a large number of great relieving arches (figure 3.8), is complex and has received much attention in the literature. See W. L. MacDonald, *The Architecture of the Roman Empire,* revised edition (Yale University Press, 1982), p. 106ff. But this construction is not carried into the dome. According to M. E. Blake and D. Taylor-Bishop, "it cannot be emphasized too strongly that the framework of the arches . . . was part of [the] wall construction and did not follow the curve of the dome. It was these relieving arches that led to so many fantastic but utterly erroneous theories of [internally ribbed] dome construction." (*Roman Construction in Italy from Nerva through the Antonines* [American Philosophical Society, 1973], p. 46.

11

K. de Fine Licht, *The Rotunda in Rome: A Study of Hadrian's Pantheon* (Copenhagen: Jutland Archaeological Society, 1968), p. 89 ff. Elastic moduli, which account for the relative rigidity of constituent materials, were estimated from empirical equations developed for lightweight modern concrete. See G. Winter and A. H. Nilson, *Design of Concrete Structures,* eighth edition (McGraw-Hill, 1972), pp. 8, 16, 26.

12

The more rigid corner of the section with the stepped rings probably induces greater bending distortion of the wall under the dome loading, and this results in somewhat larger hoop stresses within the wall.

13

MacDonald, *The Pantheon,* p. 110.

14

Alberto Terenzio, "La Restauration de Pantheon du Roma," in *La Conservation des Monuments d'Art & d'Historie* (Paris: Office International des Musées, 1934), pp. 280–285.

15

Ibid., plate XXVI. Terenzio also identifies fractures "reaching from the base of the rotunda to the summit of the dome" that he thought were brought about by differential settlement from uneven loading of the wall, particularly near the entrance of the rotunda and in the principal niche. Rather than the vertical dislocation along wall cracks that characterizes differential settlement, only traces of lateral opening across the cracks can be observed, corresponding to hoop tension.

16

This factor accounts for local openings in the wall structure as well as the effect of possible stress concentration at the boundaries of the openings.

See S. P. Timoshenko and J. N. Goodier, *Theory of Elasticity,* third edition (McGraw-Hill, 1970), p. 157ff.

17

Mario Salvadori observes that "the Pantheon . . . could only be conceived and built after the discovery of pozzolana concrete, [the thickness of which at the base of the dome] is so large that the tensile hoop stresses in it are well below the resistance of the concrete" (*Why Buildings Stand Up,* pp. 230–233). A similar observation had been made by Henry Cowan: "In the Pantheon the thickness of the concrete is so great in the lower portion of the dome that the tensile stresses are [acceptably] low." (*The Masterbuilders* [Wiley, 1977], p. 74)

18

For the calculation of thermal stress using theory given by Timoshenko and Goodier (*Theory of Elasticity,* pp. 433–437), physical properties that would generally be associated with the pozzolana described in note 9 of chapter 2 were assumed and the surface of the dome was considered to be 10°C cooler than the mass of the concrete below the surface. Differential settlements and earthquake loadings could induce additional tensile stresses; but without full records their effect is difficult to predict, and it is highly unlikely that a uniform pattern of cracks in the dome would have resulted from such loadings.

19

The segment illustrated in figure 3.14 is actually from a large-diameter annular barrel vault framing Hadrian's Teatro Marittimo. The axis of the barrel slightly curved, but the structure behaves essentially as a linear barrel vault.

20

The tensile strength of metals, for example, allowed tall structures such as the Eiffel Tower to be anchored into foundations, instead of requiring (as was necessary for all past monumental construction) great masses of masonry to ensure stability. Another consequence was the relatively sudden achievement of the new reach in building spans described in note 4.

21

Vitruvius, *The Ten Books of Architecture,* p. 46ff.

22

See W. L. Macdonald, *The Architect,* ed. S. Kostof (Oxford University Press, 1977), p. 40 ff.

23

Ward-Perkins, *Roman Imperial Architecture,* pp. 275. For background on commercial transportation in Ancient times, see J. G. Landels, *Engineering in the Ancient World* (University of California Press, 1978), pp. 133–185.

24

Ward-Perkins, *Roman Imperial Architecture,* p. 273.

25

Ibid., pp. 275–276.

26

Richard Krautheimer, *Early Christian and Byzantine Architecture,* third
edition (Penguin, 1979), p. 215ff.

27

The absence of references to theoretical solutions for *structure* in any of
the early histories of the science of mechanics is evidence of this void in
ancient engineering. See, for example, S. Sambursky, *The Physical World
of Late Antiquity* (Princeton University Press, 1962).

28

S. P. Timoshenko, *History of Strength of Materials* (McGraw-Hill, 1953),
p. 342ff.

29

An important contemporary source of events is Procopius's *On Justinian's
Buildings,* tr. H. B. Dewing, in *Buildings* (Heinman, 1940). W. Emerson
and R. L. Van Nice ("Hagia Sophia, Istanbul: Preliminary Report of a
Recent Examination of the Structure," *American Journal of Archaeology* 47
[1943], p. 412) report "the [outward] deformation of the four piers, measured at nave floor, gallery and springing of the dome arches" as "an average of 0.45 m [along the north-south axis] and 0.15 m [along the
east-west axis]." The longitudinal axis of the Hagia Sophia is not truly
east-west, but for descriptive purposes here it is assumed to be so.

30

The last campaign of major restoration was carried out by Western architects commissioned by Sultan Abdul Mecid in the middle of the
nineteenth century (Emerson and Van Nice, "Hagia Sophia," p. 406).

31

The angle at the sphere center subtended between a side of a pendentive
triangular segment and its opposite corner (see figure 3.22) is 45°. Hence,
the ratio of the dome-base diameter to that of the sphere equator should
be the cosine of 45° (0.707); but bear in mind that all these surfaces are
now much distorted. Note also that the pendentive surfaces are not tech-
nically "spherical triangles," since their sides are not formed by great
circles.

32

Robert L. Van Nice, *Saint Sophia in Istanbul: an Architectural Survey,* volume 1 (Dumbarton Oaks, 1965).

33

The failure of the buttresses was due largely to shear. The properties of
brick masonry are calculated from formulas given in Sven Sahlin's text
Structural Masonry (Prentice-Hall, 1971), p. 53ff.

34

See, e.g., David Watkin, *A History of Western Architecture* (Thames and
Hudson, 1986), p. 77. Van Nice (note 32) inferred in an earlier publication ("The Structure of St. Sophia," *Architectural Forum* [May 1963]:
135–138, 210) that the semidomes to the east and the west of the main
dome do *not* help in its support. In a later letter to *AF* (August-Septem-
ber 1964: 45–49), Van Nice reported that "these implications were rightly

questioned by . . . John Fitchen, Mario Salvadori, and Rowland Mainstone." Mainstone continues to uphold the primary structural role of the semidomes; see R. J. Mainstone, *Hagia Sophia* (Thames and Hudson, 1988), pp. 165–166.

35

Galileo Galilei, *Two New Sciences,* tr. Stillman Drake (Univesity of Wisconsin Press, 1974; Leyden: Elzevirs, 1638), p. 12ff.

36

A. A. Vasiliev, *History of the Byzantine Empire* 324–1453 (University of Wisconsin Press, 1958), p. 192.

Chapter 4

1

Abbot Suger on the Abbey Church of St-Denis and its Art Treasures, ed. and tr. E. Panofsky (second edition: G. Panofsky-Soergel) (Princeton University Press, 1979).

2

Gervase of Canterbury, "Tractatus de combustione et reparatione Cantuariensis eccelesiae," tr. R. Willis, in *The Architectural History of Canterbury Cathedral* (Longman, Pickering and Bell, 1845), pp. 32–62.

3

The Sketchbook of Villard de Honnecourt, ed. T. Bowie (Indiana University Press, 1959), plates 39–45, 47–51, 58. For commentary on these and other early drawings see Robert Branner, "Villard de Honnecourt, Reims and the origin of Gothic Architectural Drawing," *Gazette des Beaux-Arts,* sixth series, volume 61 (1963): 129–146.

4

See R. Mark, *Experiments in Gothic Structure* (MIT Press, 1982), pp. 26–31.

5

See, for example, Jean Bony, *French Gothic Architecture of the 12th and 13th Centuries* (University of California Press, 1983), p. 179ff.

6

The higher elevation of the Notre-Dame nave vaulting was drawn to my attention by L. T. Courtenay during an investigation in the summer of 1985 of the early timber roof framing above the vaults of the cathedral.

7

It was demonstrated in chapter 2 by means of dimensional analysis that interior light levels are unaffected by changing building scale. But during the course of High Gothic development, the major dimensional change between buildings took place in vaulting height. Plan dimensions remained fairly constant (compare the spans indicated by the cathedral sections in figure 4.2)—probably because of perceived structural limitations in many cases, but in other cases because of site conditions. Typical dimensions of a High Gothic central bay are 6.5 × 13.5 m (21 × 44 ft). Hence, even though the windows were enlarged, the raising of clerestories under higher-sprung vaults increased light-path lengths, and produced less favorable light-path angles to the nave floor (effectively foreshortening the window height, as described in chapter 2) that could even diminish interior light levels.

8

W. W. Clark and R. Mark, "The First Flying Buttresses: A New Recon struction of the Nave of Notre-Dame de Paris," *Art Bulletin* 67 (March 1984): 47–65. This article includes critiques of previously proposed recon-structions of the Notre-Dame nave structure by E. E. Viollet-le-Duc and M. Aubert, among others.

9

See, for example, Paul Frankl, *Gothic Architecture* (Penguin, 1962), p. 46.

10

This "learning cycle" has a parallel in our own time. The 854-m (2,800-ft) main span of the Tacoma Narrows suspension bridge, which opened in July 1940, was the third-longest in the world, and its weight per meter of roadway was by far the lightest of any long span. Tacoma Narrows epitomized the early-twentieth-century trend in suspension bridges to-ward lighter, almost ribbon-like roadway decks and slender towers; the depth of its plate-girder deck stiffening was only 1/350 of its span. Four months after the bridge opened, a fairly steady 65 km/hr (40 mph) morn-ing wind produced severe twisting oscillations in the span, which col-lapsed by midday. Soon afterward, many long-span suspension bridges built during the preiod between the two world wars, including the Bronx-Whitestone Bridge in New York and the Golden Gate Bridge in San Francisco, were stiffened by the addition of trusses to their roadway decks. And when the second Tacoma Narrows Bridge was opened a de-cade later, it too incorporated deep trusses. See Fritz Leonhardt, (MIT Press, 1984), pp. 287–289.

11

However, Branner did believe that the designers of Bourges and of Chartres learned their buttressing from the experience of Notre-Dame. See R. Branner, *La cathédrale de Bourges et sa place dans l'architecture gothique* (Tardy, 1962), pp. 163–166.

12

R. Mark, "The Structural Analysis of Gothic Cathedrals: Chartres vs. Bourges," *Scientific American* 227 (November 1972): 90–99.

13

Branner found that "the third stage of construction did not follow the lines of the original project . . . the angle of the extrados [of the higher flying buttress] would [have been] more in keeping with the angles of the lower, middle [inner aisle] roofs" (*La cathédrale de Bourges,* pp. 52–53).

14

The *Expertise* was reinterpreted by historian Alan Borg (A. Borg and R. Mark, "Chartres Cathedral: A Reinterpretation of its Structure," *Art Bul-letin* 55 [September 1973]: 367).

15

Ibid., pp. 370–371.

16

This view was almost universal. See Henri Focillon, *The Art of the West in the Middle Ages,* ed. J. Bony, second edition (Phaidon, 1969), volume 2, p. 35; P. Frankl, *Gothic Architecture,* pp. 18–19, 80, 118; Hans Jantzen, *High Gothic: The Classic Cathedrals of Chartres, Reims and Amiens* (Constable, 1962), p. 13; Nikolaus Pevsner, *An Outline of European Architecture,* seventh edition (Penguin, 1963) pp. 100–109; Charles Seymour, *Notre-Dame of Noyon in the Twelfth Century* (Yale University Press, 1939), pp. 69–71, 134–135; Whitney S. Stoddard, *Monastery and Cathedral in France* (Wesleyan University Press, 1966), pp. 130, 140, 181; Otto von Simson, *The Gothic Cathedral,* second edition (Harper and Row, 1962), pp. 205–206.

17

John Fitchen, *The Construction of Gothic Cathedrals* (Clarendon, 1961), p. 75.

18

Mark, *Experiments in Gothic Structure,* pp. 114–115.

19

Branner, *La cathédrale de Bourges,* p. 169.

20

Robert Branner, "Historical Aspects of the Reconstruction of Reims Cathedral, 1210–1241," *Speculum* 36 (1961): 23–37.

21

Bony, *French Gothic Architecture of the 12th and 13th Centuries,* pp. 271, 274.

22

Pol Abraham, *Viollet-le-Duc et la Rationalisme Médiéval* (Vincent Fréal, 1934), p. 88ff. See also chapter 2 above on the effect of pinnacle weight on buttress stability.

23

Mark, *Experiments in Gothic Structure,* pp. 52–55.

24

Robert Branner, "Le Maitre de la Cathédrale de Beauvais," *Art de France* 2 (1962): 77–92. See also Stephen Murray, "The Choir of the Church of St. Pierre, Cathedral of Beauvais: A Study of Gothic Architectural Planning and Construction Chronology in its Historical Context," *Art Bulletin* 62 (December 1980): 533–551.

25

See, for example, E. E. Viollet-le-Duc, *Dictionnaire raisoné de l'architecture française du XIe au XVIe siècle* (Librairies-Imprimeries Réunies, 1854–1868), vol. 6, p. 175.

26

Mark, *Experiments in Gothic Structure,* pp. 70–77.

27

Joseph Strayer, *On the Medieval Origins of the Modern State,* (Princeton University Press, 1970), pp. 57–58.

28

A study of the structure of the cathedral of Palma, Majorca is given in Mark, *Experiments in Gothic Structure,* pp. 92–101.

Chapter 5

1

See Catherine Wilkinson, "The New Professionalism in the Renaissance," in S. Kostof, ed., *The Architect: Chapters in the History of the Profession* (Oxford University Press, 1977).

2

See Otto von Simson, *The Gothic Cathedral* (Harper and Row, 1964), p. 23ff.

3

See Henry A. Millon, *Baroque and Rococo Architecture* (Braziller, 1965), pp. 20–23.

4

See Myra Nan Rosenfeld, "The Royal Building Administration in France from Charles V to Louis XVI," in *The Architect* (note 1), p. 176.

5

On Hooke's major contributions to the early development of the science of mechanics, see Stephen P. Timoshenko, *History of Strength of Materials* (McGraw-Hill, 1953), pp. 17–20.

6

Galileo Galilei, *Two New Sciences,* tr. S. Drake (University of Wisconsin Press, 1974; Leyden: Elzevirs, 1638).

7

Clifford Truesdell, "The Rotational Mechanics of Flexible or Elastic Bodies 1638–1788," in *Leonhard Euler: Opera Omnia,* X and XI, second series, Part 2 (Turici: Orell Füssli, 1960), p. 34.

8

Henry Wotton, *Elements of Architecture* (1624). An annotated copy of the Wotton text is known to have been in the library of Wren's father.

9

Isaac Newton, *Mathematical Principles of Natural Philosophy,* tr. A. Motte (University of California Press, 1934; London, 1686), volume 1, p. 32.

10

Stephen Wren, ed., *Parentalia, or Memoirs of the Family of Wren* (London: T. Osborn, 1750), p. 197.

11

Wren's contribution to the science of mechanics is discussed in A. R. Hall, "Mechanics and the Royal Society, 1668–70," *British Journal of the History of Science* 3 (1966–67): 30–32.

12

Kerry Downs (*The Architecture of Wren* (New [Universe Books, 1982], p. 116) writes: "In the first years of the [18th] century Wren needed to calculate, crudely by modern standards but to the limits of the knowledge of his day, a geometry at once statical and aesthetic." A second example is found on page 65 of John Summerson's *Heavenly Mansions* (Norton, 1963).

13

Robert Plot, *The Natural History of Oxfordshire,* ("printed at the theater at Oxford," 1677), pp. 274–276.

14

Eduard F. Sekler, *Wren and His Place in European Architecture* (Macmillan, 1956), p. 39.

15

Andrea Palladio, *The Four Books of Architecture* (Dover, 1965; originally published in 1570), book III, chapter VII, pp. 66–67. The form of Wren's roof structure, which follows the distribution of bending moment in the same manner as the form of the Eiffel Tower, would seem well suited to a truss designed for minimum bending. The rationale for this approach to design is discussed in R. Mark, J. K. Chiu, and J. F. Abel, "Stress Analysis of Historic Structures: Maillart's Warehouse at Chiasso," *Technology and Culture* 15 (January 1974): 56.

16

Dorn and Mark, "The Architecture of Christopher Wren," pp. 162–163.

17

Summerson, *Heavenly Mansions,* p. 65.

18

Wren noted: "The *Romans* always concealed their Butments [flying buttresses], whereas the *Normans* thought them ornamental. These, I have observed, are the first Thing that occasion the ruin of Cathedrals, being so much exposed to the Air and Weather." (*Parentalia,* p. 298)

19

See illustration in *Parentalia,* opposite p. 286.

20

Parentalia, p. 320.

21

Ibid.

22

Ibid., p. 283.

23

Viktor Fürst, *The Architecture of Sir Christopher Wren* (Lund Humphries, 1956), p. 41.

24

Somers Clark, "Saint Paul's Cathedral: Observations on Wren's System of Buttresses for the Dome Piers and on some other things," in *Sir Christopher Wren, A.D. 1632–1723* (Holder and Stoughton, 1923), pp. 73–82.

25

R. Mark, "Structural Experimentation in Gothic Architecture," *American Scientist* 66 (1978): 548–549.

26

See Howard Saalman, *Filippo Brunelleschi: The Cupola of Santa Maria del Fiore* (Zwemmer, 1980), pp. 112–134.

27

Peter Murray, *The Architecture of the Italian Renaissance* (Schocken, 1963), pp. 21–30.

28

The ongoing cracking in the Florence dome is discussed in a recent article in the *New York Times* (July 28, 1987) entitled "Cracks in a Great Dome in Florence May Point to Impending Disaster."

29

See Armando Schiavo, *La vita e Le opere architettoniche di Michelangelo* (Libreria dello Stato, 1953), p. 204. The additional chains were put into place after an investigation conducted by Giovanni Poleni in 1742: *Memorie istoriche della gran cupola del tempio vaticano, e de' danni di essa, e de' ristoramenti loro, divise in libri cinque* (Padova, 1746). Recent finite-element modeling of the Michelangelo and della Porta designs is reported in Elwin C. Robison, "St. Peter's Dome: The Michelangelo and the della Porta designs," in *Domes from Antiquity to the Present,* ed. I. Mungan (Mimar Sinan Üniversitesi, 1988), pp. 253–260.

30

Fürst, *The Architecture of Sir Christopher Wren,* pp. 105–114.

31

On the lighting of St. Paul's, Sekler observes: "The lighting of the interior is accomplished by the windows of the clerestory and the aisles, so that it is both ample and evenly distributed. Apart from the vertibule [at the western end, see plan in figure 5.7d], there are some darkened areas in the barrel-vaulted and windowless bays just before the crossing, providing a contrast which makes the dome space appear still lighter and more important." (*Wren and His Place in European Architecture,* p. 138)

32

Fürst, *The Architecture of Sir Christopher Wren,* p. 114, p. 201 (n. 512).

33

It has been suggested that Wren's design of the structural cone and the outward-tapering supporting drum below (the clear diameter is 34 m [112 ft] at the base of the drum) was guided by the experiments with catenaries performed by his architectural collaborator, Robert Hooke (note 5); but the evidence is inconclusive. See Dorn and Mark, "The Architecture of Christopher Wren," p. 173.

34

Parentalia, p. 298.

35

Ibid., pp. 352–358.

36

Wren could also have been expected to deal with theoretical aspects of interior lighting. As a professor of astronomy he had been much concerned with the developing science of optics, and he was in close communication with the two giants in this field: Isaac Newton (1642–1727), who explained most of the simple phenomena of light in terms of "corpuscle" streams, and Christopher Huygens (1629–1695), who published in

1678 a wave theory of light that was generally ignored until its acceptance in the nineteenth century. Still, the subject is never treated in Wren's notes.

Chapter 6

1

See note 14 to chapter 1.

2

Somers Clark, "Saint Paul's Cathedral: Observations on Wren's System of Buttresses for the Dome Piers and on some other things," in *Sir Christopher Wren, A.D. 1632–1723* (London: Holder and Stoughton, 1923), p. 73.

3

Marvin Trachtenberg, *The Statue of Liberty* (Viking, 1976), pp. 130–140.

4

See note 20 to chapter 1.

5

See R. Mark, "Robert Willis, Viollet-le-Duc, and the Structural Approach to Gothic Architecture," *Architectura* 7.2 (1977): 52–64.

6

To John Summerson (*Heavenly Mansions,* p. 154), Viollet-le-Duc's proposed designs "are at once unattractive and fascinating. . . . One sees that they are disciplined, daring, economical, ingenious. . . . But there is one thing missing . . . *style.*" Yet Frances H. Steiner (*French Iron Architecture* [UMI Research Press, 1894], pp. 13–14) notes that, paradoxically, France led the way in iron architecture despite the relative backwardness of her iron industry. This was because "England was entrenched in romanticism . . . [and in this milieu] the visible use of iron in public buildings was rare as the result of strenuous campaigns conducted by some of her leading architects and critics against its use. . . . Not even the most conservative French writers were unequivocally against the use of iron. . . . On the contrary, several architectural critics in France spent their lives promoting the utilization of iron in architecture . . . with an almost religious conviction."

7

E.-E. Viollet-le-Duc, *Discourses on Architecture,* tr. Henry Van Brunt (J. R. Osgood, 1875; originally published in Paris by A. Morel as *Entretiens sur l'architecture,* volume 1 in 1863 and volume 2 in 1872), volume 2 pp. 182, 186.

8

Summerson, *Heavenly Mansions,* p. 135; see also note 5 above.

9

See Sigfried Giedion, *Space, Time, and Architecture,* fifth edition (Harvard University Press, 1967), p. 206; Donald Hoffman, "Frank Lloyd Wright and Viollet-le-Duc," *Journal of the Society of Architectural Historians* 27 (1969): 173–184.

10

See Cecelia Tichi, *Shifting Gears: Technology, Literature, Culture in Modernist America* (University of North Carolina Press, 1987), p. 102ff.

11

On Maillart, see David P. Billington, *Robert Maillart's Bridges: The Art of Engineering* (Princeton University Press, 1979; on Nervi, see Pier Luigi Nervi, *Structures,* tr. G. and M. Salvadori (McGraw-Hill, 1956); on Khan, see D. P. Billington and Myron Goldsmith (eds.), *Aesthetics in the Design of Tall Buildings* (Institute for the Study of the High-Rise Habitat, Lehigh University, 1986).

12

Many historians, including Robert Branner (*Gothic Architecture* [Braziller, 1961], p. 27), have suggested that similarities in social and industrial milieu between the twelfth and the nineteenth century may explain the rise of both the High Gothic cathedral and the American skyscraper. Carl Condit has extended the analogy to the technology of their precursors: "The [early, heavily constructed] skyscraper . . . possessed a certain built-in resistance to wind, analogous to that of the Romanesque church." ("The Wind Bracing of Buildings," *Scientific American* 231 [November 1974]: 99)

13

E. Alfred Picardi, "Structural System—Standard Oil of Indiana Building," *Journal of the Structural Division, ASCE,* 99, ST4 (April 1973): 49.

14

The maximum off-center motion is about 75 cm (30 in), with a natural period (for one full cycle of motion) of about 7 seconds.

15

Marvin Trachtenberg and Isabelle Hyman, *Architecture: From Prehistory to Modernism* (Prentice-Hall/Abrams, 1986), pp. 545–546. In fairness to these authors, their earlier précis of the John Hancock Tower in Boston should also be noted; see note 6 to chapter 1.

Glossary

aedicula   A decorative niche for a statue or an image.

arcade   An array of arches on columns or piers; the arcaded lower story of a church.

apse   A semicircular or polygonal termination of the eastern end of a church.

ashlar   Square-hewn dressed stone; also, masonry in which all stones are squared, giving a uniform pattern of vertical and horizontal joints.

arch   A curved structural member, generally carrying a distributed load transverse to a line drawn between its ends, or *springing,* producing mostly internal compression. The *keystone* is the uppermost voussoir of a masonry arch. A *relieving arch* is an arch within a wall designed to relieve the wall below from the weight of the wall above. A *quadrant arch* is an internal buttress similar in form and function to an external flying buttress.

basilica   Of Roman origin, a large rectangular hall with a high central space, flanked by lower side aisles. A *basilican plan,* therefore, usually indicates three parallel rectangular aisles.

bay   Compartments into which a building is divided, normally marked by its vertical supports.

beam   A slender structural member carrying loadings transverse to its longitudinal axis, generally producing internal shear and bending moment. A *cantilever* is a beam supported at only one end. A *hammer beam* is a short horizontal timber member projecting inward from a wall and usually braced from below.

bending moment   A rotational force tending to produce curvature in a structural member.

buttress A massive upright structure, usually of masonry, that resists lateral, overturning forces (such as those transmitted by flying buttresses). An *intermediate buttress* is the slender upright support to the center of the flying buttress in a five-aisled Gothic church; a *wall buttress* is a projection attached to a wall at to enhance its stability. A *flying buttress* is an arch-like external structure that normally acts as a compression brace against lateral forces; a *spur* is a lateral wall under a side-aisle roof that acts structurally in the same manner as a flying buttress.

capital The transitional block above a column or pier.

catenary The form assumed by a hanging chain under the action of gravity. Catenary forms are normally very close to parabolic.

center of gravity A point, normally within a volume, about which the volume is balanced; hence, the weight of the volume can be taken as acting at the center of gravity.

centering Temporary shoring, usually constructed of timber, to support arches or vaulting during construction.

choir The portion of a church where services are sung, generally at the eastern end.

clerestory The wall, or story, that rises above the aisle roof, usually pierced by windows.

coffering A regular array of recessed panels in a vault or ceiling.

colonnette A light column, not usually an element of a building's primary structure.

compression An axial pushing force or stress tending to shorten a structural member.

concrete Artificial stone composed of cement, water, and *aggregates* such as crushed stone and sand. Concretes made with *hydraulic cement,* which combines chemically with water, can be used for underwater construction.

course A line of stone blocks. *Coursed* masonry is composed of lines of blocks, but it may contain *broken courses* when the joints are not all in the same plane.

crossing The space formed by the central piers at the intersection of the longitudinal and lateral axes in a cruciform-plan church.

dead weight The self-weight of a structure.

dome Usually an axisymmetric structure of arched section forming a ceiling or roof. A *semi-dome* is half a *hemispherical dome* or a dome having a semicircular cross section. *Step rings* are the concentric, projecting rings often placed around the base of a dome.

drum A cylindrical or polygonal wall supporting a dome or a lantern.

footing The projecting base of a pier or wall that distributes loadings to the subsoil.

frame A skeletal load-bearing structure. A *rigid frame* is a planar assembly of beam-like elements rigidly connected to one another, generally formed of timber in early construction and of steel or reinforced concrete in large-scale modern construction.

gallery In a church, the roofed or vaulted space over the side aisle forming a second story above the arcade story.

hemicycle   The semicircular structure of the rounded termination of a church.

lantern   A small open-walled tower on the top of a dome or roof to admit light to the space below.

light intensity   The measure of light emission from a natural or artificial source. *Illuminance* is the measure of surface brightness. *Light-path length* is the distance from a source to an illuminated surface.

meridian   A radial-in-plan generating line of a dome surface.

modeling   Modeling techniques are used in engineering to solve for deformations and for force and stress distributions in complex structures. *Physical modeling* involves taking measurements, usually from a small scale model, which are *scaled* to give the response of a *prototype* full-scale structure. In *photoelastic* modeling, these measurements are derived from optical interference patterns using polarized light. In *numerical modeling,* the abstracted material properties, geometry, and loading of the prototype are programmed into an electronic computer. In *finite-element* (numerical) modeling, the prototype form is represented by a series of coordinates taken at finite intervals on its surface.

mullion   A light, upright division member within a window.

nave   The main portion or central aisle of a church, the western end of which is generally devoted to the lay worshipper.

pendentive   A triangular segment of vaulting at the base of a dome, usually used for transition from a round-plan to a square-plan space.

pier   An upright structure of masonry acting mainly to support vertical loads.

pinnacle   A small spire, usually surmounting a buttress or a roof.

principal rafter   A sloping beam from the ridge of the roof to the wall; it provides primary support to longitudinal *purlins,* which in turn support the lighter *common rafters* of the roof.

reactions   The internal forces acting at the supports of a loaded structure.

rotunda   A circular hall, usually topped with a dome.

shear   A force or stress acting transverse to the axis of a structural member and tending to cause sliding between its constituent elements.

stability   The capacity of a structure to remain in stable equilibrium under the action of applied forces.

stiffness   A measure of a structure's resistance to deformation.

strain   A measure of local deformation within a structure.

strain gauge   A device used to measure strain, usually by measuring the change in resistance of a small electrical element cemented to the surface of the structure under study.

strength   The level of stress that causes a material to fail.

stress   A measure of the local intensity of internal force within a structure.

strut   A light, slender structural member that resists compressive force along its axis.

surcharge   The mass placed over the haunches of an arch or vault to enhance stability.

template   A pattern used to establish the profile of cut stone—used also to profile photoelastic models.

tension   An axial stretching force or stress tending to elongate a structural member.

tie beam   A main horizontal member of a timber roof truss that acts in tension to prevent the roof from spreading. It does not normally function primarily as a beam.

tracery   Curving ornamental mullions of stone set into medieval windows.

transept   The transverse arms of a cruciform-plan church, usually forming a separation between the choir and the nave.

triforium   The wall passage above the arcade story and below the clerestory in a mature Gothic church.

truss   An assembly of struts and ties generally forming triangles and carrying loadings applied transverse to its horizontal axis.

vault   A ceiling or roof structure of arched section. A *barrel vault* is a continuous vault of semicircular section. A *groined vault* is formed by the intersection of two orthogonal barrel vaults, the *groins* being the lines of intersection. *Quadripartite vaulting* divides each bay into four compartments; *sexpartite vaulting* divides each pair of bays into six compartments. *Ribs* are the arches that project from below the vault's surface. The *webbing* is the stone surface of a vault seen as infilling between the ribs.

voussoir   Wedge-shaped stone used as a building block of a masonry arch or vault.

Index